Holistic singing and toning.

Developing voice power for healing and enjoyment.

"A book to help those who love to sing."

D1827574

First published November 1998.
Reprinted (in part) April 2001

© Copyright by Richard Rigby.

National Library of Australia - Cataloguing in Publication Data.
ISBN 0646334735

Published in Australia by Richard Rigby
Kenmore Specialist Centre
2081 Moggill Road, Kenmore, Queensland, 4069, Australia.

Typeset and printed by
Merino Litho Pty Ltd
18 Baldock Street
Moorooka Qld 4105

Holistic singing and toning

Developing voice power for healing and enjoyment

By Dick Rigby
Clinical Psychologist and Voice Therapist

Acknowledgements

Thank you to the many wonderful people who have helped me reach the stage where I was able to summon the courage and determination to write this, my first book. My wife Jenny has been supportive and helpful through the conception, gestation, labour and birth of this book. My dear friend Pat Lleiss has given support, encouragement, knowledge and energy.

Also, I have been inspired by the speakings and writings of Pia Mellody, as well as Hal and Sidra Stone. I was lucky enough to meet with these people. Thanks to my good friend and colleague Roz Nutting who is always an inspiration, and a legend in her time. My thanks to Chris Campbell for his help with references and contacts in relation to Balinese music. Chris and Jenny James have been an inspiration with their teachings and knowledge.

For the skilled and careful proof reading, thank you to Jacqui, Michelle, Gina, and Kerrin. Thank you to Charlie Scandrett for his valuable editorial comment.

To the many more that I have not mentioned, thank you for your help and support.

Dedication

To my beautiful
wife Jenny

Contents

Preface

You don't have to be a good singer or speaker to benefit from reading this book. But, hopefully by the time you have finished you will know how to go about becoming a better singer or speaker.

If you don't already know it, I hope to convince you that you don't have to be a "good" singer to enjoy singing.

Our journey towards the joy of singing and toning involves reducing unreasonable fear.

Introduction

The "logic" of fear

Many people want to learn how to sing better and enjoy their voice. It is nearly always fear that stops them. Much of the first half of this book is about how this fear is set up in the first place and how it can be cured.

Case study:– Pamela

Pamela was 16 years old when the incident occurred. She was shy, highly strung and prone to worry about things. She had a really beautiful singing voice and was a member of the school choir. Much was expected of her because of her outstanding musical talent.

One morning, she was due to sing a solo before the school assembly. She was feeling a bit nervous before it came her time to sing. As she stood before the assembly, the piano began to play the introduction to her song. Her mind went into a whirl. She began to feel a deep sense of panic form in the pit of her tummy. She felt a panic attack starting.

When it came her moment to sing, she burst into tears.

Her singing teacher came forward and comforted Pamela and helped her from the stage. Pamela felt ashamed and humiliated by the experience. She blamed herself for being such an idiot. She had made a fool of herself in front of her peers, teachers and the whole school. Pamela could not be consoled.

From that day on, she refused to sing in public, so great was her sense of humiliation and fear.

Pamela's parents were very concerned about her and they brought her to see me for help. I asked Pamela if she wanted my help to overcome her fear of singing in public. She said "No thanks". "If you cure me of my fear of singing, I will have to sing on assembly again and the same thing will happen."

Such simple "logic" backed up with such an intensity of terror wiped out her ability to make the rational assessment of the situation. She was unable to understand that if she overcame her fear of singing in public, then she wouldn't have another panic attack, and history would not repeat itself.

The story has a happy ending. Several years later, Pamela returned for help. She was able to overcome her fear of singing in public. She completed a Bachelor of Music at University and began a career of part time professional singing.

She now really enjoys her public performances.

By overcoming her fear of singing in public, Pamela began to learn to use her singing voice as a wonderfully powerful force for self expression, creativity, joy and healing.

> *Many people who could enjoy singing, believe that they have a terrible voice. This belief stops them from knowing the joys of sharing their voice with others.*

Several years ago, I began helping people overcome their fears of singing and other forms of vocal expression such as public speaking. I have been able to help people change from a position of almost total terror to a position of confidence with their voice. It is such a buzz for me to play a part in their recovery. Ordinary people can learn to experience the joy and fun of singing confidently for the first time in their adult life.

For some people, learning to sing and speak out with confidence has changed their lives in terms of the way they deal with other people.

A book about learning to sing with confidence

I wanted to write a book that taught people how to sing and speak with confidence. This is it.

If you are either an amateur or professional singer who has some problem with your singing voice, then this book should be helpful. However, it will also be of help if you believe that you "can't sing a note" and you want to learn how to start.

Most of what is contained in this book applies just as much to improving your speaking voice as it does to your singing voice.

The book gives advice and guidelines on how to breathe more effectively and in a healthier way. Breath is the foundation of the quality of the singing and speaking voice.

Even some professional speakers or singers have problems with vocal expression from time to time. This book provides guidelines and advice for overcoming these problems. The problems may be stage fright, or posture problems. Many other issues can arise that effect the voice.

You will be introduced to voice toning. Toning is the use of sustained notes to help with psychological and physical healing and voice development. Toning is also used to facilitate the integration of psychological processes. Toning can be just for fun and enjoyment.

An example of toning would be making an "oo" sound with your voice for one or two minutes.

Singing and toning can be enjoyable, fun and can lead to spiritual enrichment.

We can learn how to use our voices as a force for healing ourselves and others. We can even use our voices to make a chorus to heal the planet.

Singing and toning are wonderful vehicles for bringing people together.

Singing and toning can lead to people feeling more empowered to speak their own truth.

I wanted to write a book that gave you, the reader hope and optimism for the future.

I believe I have done this.

How the book began

Some of my clients have asked me to recommend a book that would help them develop their voice strength. I wasn't able to find an "easy to read" and comprehensive book on the subject. There were some self help books that teach how to sing (check out the bibliography) but there appeared to be none that were easy to read and dealt with both the psychology of healing the voice and the using of the voice as a tool to heal.

The idea of writing a book about voice development had been fermenting in my brain for a couple of years. At the beginning of 1998, I took the awesome decision to write this book, and I first put "finger to word processor" in February.

Music and psychotherapy have been two major passions in my life, so it came as no surprise that my interests in music, voice development and therapy began to converge.

I have worked as a professional musician and singer for many years preforming folk, jazz and mainstream music. In the mid 1980s

I even became involved in stand up comedy work. The various experiences that I gained in music and comedy became assets that I have used in my therapy work with the voice. Humour is an essential element to all therapy, but it is particularly effective with voice work.

Also during the 1980s, I ran several music therapy groups for psychiatric in-patients. These groups were very helpful in improving these patients' self confidence and sense of grounding.

Several years ago, I attended an inspirational workshop run by Chris James in my home town of Brisbane, Australia. The workshop was about Voice Toning and voice development. This was my first encounter with the concept of toning. I was so impressed that I attended a one week residential workshop a couple of months later.

I began to apply these new techniques of toning in my practice. At the same time, I began running workshops on singing, toning and voice development. I was surprised at the amount of interest the workshops generated. People really wanted to learn about three aspects in particular:–

1. How to improve the quality of their voice.
2. How to overcome fears of singing or speaking.
3. How to use their voice for healing of self and others.

Some of the people who attended these workshops were more interested in the first two aspects, while other people were more interested in learning how they could use toning and other techniques as instruments of healing.

The feedback from these workshops has been good from nearly all participants. Most people came away feeling much more empowered with the use of their voice, and learned many ways for developing their voices. The few people who were disappointed were expecting just singing lessons and found the psychological stuff a bit hard to deal with.

The exercises and techniques that I use on these workshops are covered in this book.

Selecting a book title – Why holistic?

The approach that I use in my therapy is holistic. That means the therapy takes account of the interaction of mind, body and spirit. The holistic principles apply to both healing the voice, and to using the voice as an instrument of healing.

This book is about the therapies that I have found to be most effective.

As I searched for a title for this book, the label "Holistic Singing and Toning" superglued itself to my mind.

Moving from technical to holistic singing

For some people singing is just a technical exercise. For these people, singing is little more than the act of filling the lungs with air and then vibrating the vocal chords as they push the air out to make a singing sound. Unfortunately, even today, some singing teachers are too focussed on this technical level.

Sad but true!

The flip side of the coin is the singer who is connected to his or her feelings. Their music comes alive.

Some singing teachers have a passion for singing, and this passion comes through in their teaching. Several years ago, I was lucky enough to be taught by such a teacher. Most singing teachers encourage their students to put some feeling into what they sing.

This is a good thing.

However, singing and toning can be even more than this. For that matter, any form of the vocal expression can be more than just this. Holistic singing is a term I thought up, to capture the idea of integration and wholeness. "Holistic singing" is about the integration of the voice with body, mind, soul and spirit. (An explanation for soul and spirit is given in chapter 15).

To some people, holistic singing could mean even more than this. It could mean our connectedness with all matters in the universe; stars, galaxies and black holes.

black holistic singing

Don Campbell (1992a) refers to the holistic approach to music in the following way.

> *"The sense of holistic relevance can be classified in religious, social, psychological and neurobiological terms, but not in musical terms until the awareness of music's elemental connection to all of life's rhythm is observed from a deep well of our elemental memory. That experience can be compared to the holy, the spirit filled, the complete gestalt or zenith of awareness and function." "The holistic key is one of constant awareness, not just knowledge, of the exciting and wonderful creativity that exists in all life".*

Connected by voice

Our voices can connect us with all things; inanimate and animate. In this book, I have particularly focussed on the connections that the voice can make with our bodies, minds and spirit. Singing and toning can become part of what we do and who we are. Not only that, the voice can be a resource to allow us to reach deep into our psyche and to connect with unknown parts. We can use this connection to learn and to heal. Through the voice connecting us with these parts inside us, we can communicate with, and learn to listen to these parts.

You're the Voice (Song)

You're the voice try and understand it
Make a noise and make it clear
Wah-oh-oh-oh, wah-oh-oh-oh
We're not going to sit in silence
We're not going to live in fear
Wah-oh-oh-oh, wah-oh-oh-oh

A Qunta, C Thompson, K Reid, M Ryder.

The voice can also connect us with parts outside ourselves. With our voice we can both give and receive as we connect with other people and things.

Healing with the voice

As I have said, music and singing are instruments for holistic healing because they reach to all parts of the mind and body. In part B of this book, I will talk more about how toning has special healing qualities. I will talk about how holistic singing and toning are used to raise our level of energy.

Singing and toning can be used to raise our awareness of ourselves and the things that are going on around us. We can use this to better connect us with the joy of living.

Case study:– **Rebecca**

The healing power of sound can be illustrated in the story of Rebecca: Rebecca was 29 years old when she first sought help for her problems with anxiety and agoraphobia. She dreaded going

shopping and when she did she was in constant fear of having a panic attack. For her, a panic attack was a very unpleasant experience, feeling as if she was in real danger. She didn't even know what was the cause of the panic attacks.

She had tried relaxation therapy but it didn't help at the time she was having a panic attack. She said; " No matter what I do, I just can't get back in control". However, when she first learned about toning, she found that it helped sooth her anxiety. She found that she was able to use toning as part of her morning meditation. She used a deep note to tone with and this seemed to make a profound connection in her mind.

As time went by, she became more and more skilled at using the toning meditation and began to make use of it in public places. She would make sure that her toning was at a very low volume so that no one else around could hear her. The toning gave her a calming focus and helped her slow down her breathing.

Using this method, Rebecca learned to manage her panic attacks even in crowded shopping centres.

When we are ill, music and singing can assist us with our return to health. When we are healthy, music and singing are about capitalizing on that health with feelings of wellbeing.

While I am getting a bit carried away here, let me say that; "Your whole body can resonate to a holistic symphony of vibrations and sounds." Holistic singing and toning is about healthy life-style, physical health, psychological wellbeing, personal power, harmonious relationships and harmony with the planet.

What more could you want?

Sound bonding from parent to child

Most of this book is devoted to fixing up our voice problems that have been caused or contributed to by someone else; usually by an adult at the time we were a child. That is the lot of therapy. Once we are adult, it is our responsibility to heal our own problems no matter how these problems were set up in the first place.

A child's early experience with sound is very important in the formation of a good relationship with his or her voice. The sound and rhythm contact between the mother and child while the child is still in the womb are important. In the early post natal months, this sound and rhythm contact between the mother and the new born infant is also vitally important.

Our voice is shaped by our early experiences. How these early experiences shape us is partly determined by our temperament. Let me tell you the story of two children, Johnny and Myrtle. The reason we were told that Johnny stopped singing in primary school was because his choir master told him to, "Be quiet and just mime the words and let the kids who can sing do the singing". It is true that this was said, but it does not tell the whole story. Johnny may well have been very upset and even traumatised by this event, but the same thing happened to Myrtle and it didn't stop her from singing.

The teachers' comments were traumatic for Johnny but not for Myrtle. The explanation for this is that Johnny and Myrtle had different temperaments and different home environments.

It is the context of the trauma, as well as the trauma itself that determines whether or not any negative effects will be lasting. Johnny didn't get support and encouragement from home but Myrtle did. This made the difference to the way each child dealt with the teacher's comments.

I believe if the home is loving, connected and supportive, kids can survive most of the negative stuff handed out to them at school.

When trauma is lodged deep in the psyche, and that stops you enjoying singing, then it's time to get it fixed. That is what this book is about.

An invitation

Use this book to develop your voice power. Use it to integrate and to heal. And don't forget to have some fun while you are doing it.

PROTOCOLS

A. GENDER REFERENCES

One can never please everyone with the "he and she" generic terms. So I have decided, on a quite arbitrary basis, to refer to all therapists as female and all clients as male. Apologies to all male therapists and female clients.

The singing and public speaking performer I have arbitrarily called a "he". Again, my apologies to all female performers.

B. THERAPIST-CLIENT NAME PROTOCOLS

I have had some difficulty working out what generic terms to use that cover the range of different therapist and client situations. So I have adopted the following protocols:

The term *therapist* is interchangeable with the following terms:– Workshop leader, workshop facilitator, psychotherapist, healer, giver of toning, teacher, and guru who knows everything there is to know.

The term *client* is interchangeable with the following terms:– Patient, sound recipient (or receiver), student, psycho-pilgrim and workshop participant.

C. MOTHER-FATHER PROTOCOLS

I have referred to the primary care giver for a child as the "mother", particularly where the child is young. However, the primary care giver could be the father or a grandparent or equally divided among two or more care givers.

D. PARTNER PROTOCOLS

I have referred to the person who does voice exercises with you as your partner. This person may be a singing teacher, a therapist, a spouse, a friend or the local vicar.

E. CASE STUDIES AND PRIVACY

I have changed the names of all clients that I have quoted as case studies and where necessary have changed non essential information in order to protect the privacy of the client.

F. DISCLAIMER

Nowhere in this book do I make a claim that toning is a sole magic cure for any physical ailment or condition. What I do say is that toning does seem to help in the treatment of various physical ailments and conditions. There is solid scientific evidence to support the healing power of various forms of sound therapy. I also believe that toning has few, if any, adverse side effects. I have witnessed how singing and toning can improve a person's sense of confidence and well being. Most of us know that improving a person's sense of confidence and wellbeing can lead to an improvement in a physical ailment.

I have also witnessed how various exercises described in this book can be helpful.

PART A

Learning to sing and tone

I really want to sing

Children love to sing.
Some of us have lost that love.
We need to claim it back.

For most of us, "good singing" is like the image of a slim young woman's body in a glossy fashion magazine. So "beautiful" yet so unattainable. Singing well and confidently appears to be out of reach. The advent of the electronic media has made matters worse.

Every day we hear the beautiful voices of professional singers thanks to the electronic media. We hear them on the radio, on TV, background music at the shopping centres etc. The airways are full of singers with beautiful voices. And most of us say, "I wish I could sing like that, but I never will be able".

As recorded music has become more and more popular this century, we have learned to compare ourselves with professional singers rather than with our peers. What chance do most of us have with such tough comparisons?

The early days: Family sing-alongs

Before electronic home entertainment became popular, and particularly before TV, families used to provide their own entertainment. Sometimes families gathered around the piano for a family "sing-along". Also, attendances at church were higher in the early days and people sang there as well. Singing was a participant activity.

Even when I grew up in the 1950s, family sing-alongs were still happening. Now they seem to be a rare event. In those days, records and record players were relatively expensive and out of the reach of many families.

Before popular recorded music, hearing someone with a really good voice would be an uncommon occurrence compared with today. Either we would have to go to a concert as a special treat or Aunt Florence would come over and give one of her recitals. A professional quality voice was a special treat. I have heard it said so often from members of my parent's generation that, " When we were kids we made our own entertainment".

In a family I knew several years ago, the father was keen on family sing-alongs and he loved to organize his adult children, and anyone else into rounds singing songs such as "London's Burning". But there was little or no enthusiasm from the rest of his family. The family would go along with these sing-alongs at Christmas. However, the mother, in particular, set high standards and was very judgmental. The adult children learned to internalize these judgements and this robbed them of their joy of singing.

In very recent years, the tide appears to be turning. There seems to be a return to singing for pleasure. More and more people seem to be developing an interest in singing, in particular, choral singing, karioke, chanting and toning. Paul Newham (1998) talks about a revival in community singing particularly in England, including choirs being formed to recapture the beautiful and haunting Gregorian Chants.

I think that this development is partly an outcome of the personal growth movement. Singing is a form of joyful self expression. People want to express their new found power and freedom in the form of singing.

I really want to sing

Once you make the decision that "I really want to sing", the task of learning how to improve our singing voice presents itself. This task has two parts:–

1. Overcoming any psychological blocks to vocal expression.
2. Training or retraining the voice.

Fear of singing and negative labels

Many people have a fear of singing. We weren't born with that fear; we learned it. If we have a fear of performing in front of other people, that fear can be called performance anxiety.

The first thing to do to reduce performance anxiety is to start to change some of the language that we apply to singing. So often the terms "good voice" and "bad voice" are applied. We understand that a "good voice" is one that is pleasing to the ear, and a "bad voice" is one that isn't.

However, these terms as applied to singing, are misleading because they can imply that your voice is that way and it is going to stay that way. I don't mind the term "good voice" but I would rather have the term "bad voice" replaced with "untrained or undeveloped voice".

This leaves the door open for learning and improving the voice.

Another example of negative labelling is the term "tone deaf". Many clients who come to me for voice development, say that they are "tone deaf". More often than not, when I test them for pitch recognition, I find that they have a good sense of pitch. They have not yet learned how to make the necessary connections and corrections between the mouth, the ear and the vocal chords. More about this voice tuning process later.

I suppose there are people who are tone deaf, but I have not met any yet. Don Campbell (1997) says that; "In teaching several thousand of students over the years, I have not found a single one who cannot match the sound or the harmony of the sound within a few minutes".

Genetics vs environment

Nobody knows exactly the relative part that genetics and environment play in how good a voice we have as adults. Each plays its part. But whatever we were given genetically, it is up to us to develop and strengthen our voice to reach its potential. Even if our environment has been unkind to us by way of physical disease that effects our voice, or negative judges of our voice, it is still up to us to do the remedial work if we want to sing or speak with skill.

For those with a gifted voice

I believe that nearly all of us were born with beautiful voices. In many cases, our voices were messed up by certain key adults, or by disease or injury. It is the task of a voice remedial therapist to recognise and develop the beauty and strength in our voices. It is also their task to help us overcome our hangups or handicaps.

A few people are lucky enough to be born with a particularly gifted voice. One would imagine that for one so lucky their singing problems would be over. However, for those people, their life journey is not necessarily easier than those with less than outstanding voice, it is just different.

We children were all born with beautiful voices.
Why did the adults have to mess them up?

Being born with a gifted voice is just the start. For that singing voice to develop with quality and strength, the child has to grow up in a supportive and nurturing environment.

More often than not, he child growing up with the gifted voice will be made a fuss of and asked to perform in public at an early age. Such children may grow up with confidence in their singing voice or they may grow up with problems. But more about these gifted people later.

For those with a less than gifted voice

For those few gifted people among us who can sing like a bird. Good for them. But for the rest of us, our voices range from croaky to ordinary to quite pleasant. Whatever the quality of the voice we are born with, our life's journey from the womb to the grave will shape how our voice develops and how confident we feel about our voice.

"Our personal association with our voice
has a history of a lifetime."
Pat Lleiss (1998).

How we feel about our voice will depend on whether the key influential people in our lives were nurturing and supportive or whether they were critical or indifferent.

OUR SINGING JUDGES

After we are born, we begin the life long journey of running the gauntlet of "singing judges". Our singing judges are like the judges of a boxing match, and our experiences are like the rounds in the boxing ring. Our voice ability and voice confidence is shaped by these judges. Their judgements can be either supportive or damaging. I have given examples below of how negative judgements in particular can damage self confidence.

Let us look at the various rounds and what happens when something goes wrong in each round.

Preparation for round one: From conception to birth. The womb sound.

In the security of the womb, we are free of judgements about the quality of our voice. Because we can't make a vocal sound, we are just passive receivers of sound.

The fetus can receive sound. Campbell (1997) describes how the ear of the fetus becomes functional after 18 weeks and actively listens from 24 weeks on. Our earliest experiences with sound are the perception of sound vibrations transmitted through the wall of the uterus.

I am sure that sound can have a profound effect on the developing fetus. The prebirth environment can be nurturing and safe. Sound can become associated with safety and pleasure. Campbell (1997) also describes how the fetus will react differently to different forms of music. Certain forms of classical music will calm, and certain forms of rock music will activate the baby.

If the womb is bombarded with loud jarring sounds, this would most likely have an adverse effect on the fetus. Also, if the womb environment is contaminated with cigarette and alcohol toxins, no matter what the sound that the fetus hears, that sound may have unpleasant and fearful associations.

Round one. From birth to preschool

The first of these judges is our primary care giver or givers. All except a very few babies are born with a voice. Our birth is our first chance to make a sound and hear what we sound like. From the moment we make that first sound, we will be influenced by the effect that sound has on other people.

We know a fair bit about how important the very early years are in the healthy development of the infant. We know how important touch is. We know how important eye contact between the mother and the infant is. ("Mother" is the name I give to the primary care giver). We know something about how important sound is in developing the bond between the mother and the child. There is still so much more to learn.

In the first months of life an infant learns to use his voice to communicate. He learns when his voice causes pleasure for others and when it causes displeasure. In these very early years, the infant's mother (and others) shape the way the baby begins to feel about his voice.

Very young babies are capable of producing melodic sounds in the form of gurgling, or soft sustained notes. If a baby is encouraged to make these melodic sounds by, say the mother smiling and imitating the sounds, the baby is rewarded and encouraged to keep making the sound.

Don Campbell says that:–

"Baby talk is far more musical than general speech. That the intonation may be more communicative than the words is intuitive. The first musical fragments produced by children occur from the twelfth to fifteenth month. They may not have any tuneful identity, but their undulating patterns over small intervals do show signs of the descending minor third. A quantum leap occurs around the age of one and a half, when children begin to use seconds, thirds and fourths in their singing patterns, although the intervals are not particularly tuned to the musical ear."

At these early stages of voice development in the child, the rudiments of self esteem regarding voice production are being established. Some might say that the infant is too young to understand whether or not he has a good voice. But, in simple terms the child is on a behavioural reinforcement schedule, just like Pavlov's dogs with the bell. The infant learns quickly.

Pavarotti's operatic conditioning

I believe that round one is very important in voice development particularly where negative messages are given.

Round two. Preschool years

These years are also very important to both the development of confidence and to developing singing skills. An example will illustrate the damage that a critical parent can do at this stage.

David grew up in a family that was critical of his singing from an early age. His father would say "shut that racket up." "If you want to sing, go away and make the noise somewhere else". David really didn't have much chance. When he was three years old, he loved to sing. By the time he started school, he would only sing very quietly and then only when the other children were singing.

Round three. Early school years

These years should be the formative years when children learn to really enjoy singing and using their developing voices. Margaret was luckier than David. She had a supportive family and got through round one ok. When she was very young, her mother would say, "Darling you have a really beautiful voice and I am sure you are going to grow up one day to become a famous singer". Margaret thrived on this praise. In her preschool years, Margaret got lots of encouragement for her singing and even gave family concerts.

She hit the skids at round two. When she went to school, she would sing out loudly and confidently. She just couldn't understand why the other children would tease her and tell her to shut up.

After several months of torment and confusion, she decided that her parents must have got it wrong and she really did have a horrible voice. From that point on she stopped singing confidently and would only mouth the words when she had to sing with the class in school.

She carried that belief system through to her adult life and only started to question it when she reached her early forties. At this age she began to train her voice and joined a choir. She recaptured the love and passion that she had for singing as a child.

The two singing teachers

My wife Jenny is a year one teacher. In one primary school where she taught there was a music teacher who took the year one children. This teacher wanted to teach the children how to sing

"properly". She was shaping these 5 and 6 year old children so that in the future they would be part of the school choir, which was well known in the district for winning eisteddfods.

She put a good deal of emphasis on singing in tune. When one of the children was not in tune she would draw attention to this child and correct them. She also wanted to teach the children voice control so she had the children sing in a controlled way. The children felt under pressure to perform. They didn't enjoy her classes and when the classes were over they would feel tired and have low energy.

Then along came this young newly graduated teacher. He wanted the kids to have fun. He encouraged them to sing loudly and didn't worry if someone was out of tune. He got the kids to sing fun songs about spaghetti and to make the slurping sounds as they sucked the spaghetti in. The kids loved his classes and looked forward to them. There would always be lots of fun and energy in his classes.

These two music teachers had vastly contrasting styles of music teaching. Both teachers wanted to develop musical skills in the children and both were well intended. The first teacher's style emphasized skills teaching. The graduate teacher's style was to fire the kids with enthusiasm and then to subtly introduce skills development.

Both teachers may have achieved the same result in the end, but with the experienced music teacher, most kids lost their passion and interest in singing. With the graduate teacher, the kids learned that music was for enjoyment and this provided a motivational basis.

Round four. Mid school years

Harry got through round one and two successfully. He had supportive parents. His father had once been in an amateur light opera company and wanted to encourage Harry to sing. By the time Harry got to school, he was a confident singer and had a reasonable quality voice. His grade one teacher was very supportive and most of the other kids were not negative about his singing.

In grade six, he hit round three. He did not get on with his teacher and the teacher was a very critical type of person. This teacher made critical comments about Harry's singing and the children took the opportunity to join in and rubbished Harry about his voice.

Harry was very confused about the mixed messages that he was getting from home and school. It didn't stop him from singing, but it severely dented his confidence. It wasn't until he joined a choral society during his university days that he began to regain his confidence.

Round five. Change of voice at puberty

Julian enjoyed his primary school years and was always in the school choir. He would sometimes sing the soprano role as a solo. When he reached secondary school certain changes started to happen to his voice. He no longer had control over his pitch and tone. He would attempt to sing a note and his voice would crack. He found this very embarrassing. This coincided with an age of heightened sensitivity to self image.

Julian was also a bit of a perfectionist and he could not stand the loss of control over the quality of his voice.

He went to his singing teacher and got bad advice. The singing teacher said that many boy sopranos lost the ability to sing properly when their voices began to break. Julian was very discouraged and stopped singing and never attempted to retrain his voice to his new register.

The advice was bad because it took away hope. The voice is an instrument that one learns to play. Julian could have retrained his voice to the new register. After all he had all that background in voice training. His singing teacher should have said that it is like going from trumpet to trombone; it takes a bit of time to get used to the new register.

Boys' voices drop as much as an octave at puberty. Girls' voices also may drop, but only a matter of several tones.

Round six. The teenage cringe

I suppose that teenagers have always been judgmental since time began. But it seems that in Australia today, teenagers are very judgmental of the singing voice. I remember several years ago, how I used to teach secondary school music in a combined boy's and girl's school. I would ask a class in lower secondary school;

"How many of you can sing above average?". Three hands would go up.

"How many can sing about average?" Another five hands would go up.

Finally, "How many can sing below average?" The other 23 hands would go up.

These were not music students, they were main stream classes. This ratio was very consistent between various classes. The group that were below average were always by far the biggest. There was no objectivity in these kid's judgement of themselves. In a specialist singing class, the ratios were different, as you would expect.

Children learned to devalue their own voices. What are the pressures on children that make them so self critical, and how are these values learned?

One of the pressures on the children was the tall poppy syndrome. The syndrome is that children who wish to excel in Australian schools are often ridiculed by their peer groups. Many of the children in the school that I taught came from social backgrounds that held strong anti-tall-poppy sentiments.

Round seven. The adult experience
Case study:– Musical Maria

In my experience, it is not as common that an adult person will have a major loss of confidence in their voice. But it can happen. Maria enjoyed singing. She worked as a secretary during the day and would sing with a band one or two evenings a week. The work was mainly for clubs and pubs and it required a fairly strong voice.

At 23 years of age, Maria broke up with her long term boy friend and went through a really rough time. One night she was singing on stage and her voice just gave out. It changed from a strong voice to a really wispy voice. She "died on stage". As luck would have it, it was a rough audience that night and they gave her a hard time.

She felt deeply traumatised by that experience. She felt so humiliated that she refused to sing in public again.

It wasn't until years later that she understood that her voice had given out because of all the personal difficulties that she was going through at the time. Maria worked in therapy to overcome the trauma of this experience and the inhibitions that this trauma had produced in her voice. After this work, she was able to return to a part time singing career which she enjoyed.

The Survivors

Many people who come to my workshops have grown up with negative judgements about their voices from parents, peers, siblings and even teachers. But they say, "I really want to sing". I love to hear a person say this because I know that if their motivation is strong enough, they can overcome the blocks which stop them enjoying singing. It doesn't mean that they can become a "very good singer", it just means that they are good enough to enjoy singing without shame and embarrassment.

Learning how to sing as an adult can be learning how to rediscover the voice that you lost as a child. The influences of the various negative judges in the rounds can be overcome.

It's well worth the effort.

If an adult doesn't overcome his or her hangups and negativity about singing, they are likely to pass them on to the next generation. I think that's a crime.

Motivators to learn singing

There are two main motivators for people to learn the skills of singing:–

1. The determination to acquire skills. The obsessional student does well here. He practises for hours in order to perfect the technique. Such students may develop a singing style without "soul" because of their preoccupation with technique. Some of these students have been forced to learn singing (or some other musical instrument) in order to fulfil an ambition of a parent.

2. The desire to learn to sing because of the love of music. This student learns to sing with passion. They may or may not have the patience to practise and learn the correct techniques for voice control, but they love to sing.

For some people, there is the combination of both motivators. A student with a balance between the two is motivated by passion and loves to sing, but also has the discipline to perfect techniques. These are necessary ingredients for a top professional singer.

Let us have another look at the example of the two teachers, I believe that the graduate teacher's style did nothing to prevent the development of quality singing. However, the regular teacher's style did take the enjoyment and therefore the motivation out of singing for the children.

CHAPTER 2

Physical and Psychological Influences

Many things can stop us using our pure voice.
Some are physical and others psychological.
Most are a mixture of both.

Let us look at the relative contribution of physical and psychological influences that prevent our voices from reaching their potential.

PHYSICAL CONDITIONS

Physical causes of voice problems may include, neuromuscular diseases, obstructive growths, nodules, polyps, abnormal folds, a variety of congenital conditions, and scar tissue left over from injury or disease. Aronson (1990) describes a variety of voice disorders under the headings of congenital, inflammation, tumors, endocrine disorders, trauma and neurologic disease.

The voice box is a very complex organ and is sensitive to damage. Damage to the voice box may be caused by an impact to the throat, or by a severe infection or burning of the throat.

Many singers, both amateur and professional, suffer from hoarseness of the throat from time to time. Reflux of gastric juices can cause hoarseness. Fortunately this condition is usually very easily treated with medication. Hoarseness can also be a side effect of certain medication such as corticosteroid treatment for asthma. If in doubt about possible side effects of medication, check with your doctor or pharmacist.

Problems with voice production can also be caused by interference with the supply of air to the vocal chords. Interference with air flow can be caused by a narrowing of the airways such as that caused by asthma. Air flow may also be restricted by airway obstructions such as a growth. Restricted breath control also may be caused by impaired muscular control.

In my work with clients, I have found that most problems with restricted air passage or control of air flow are caused by poor posture and breathing habits. In chapter 7, I will discuss ways of improving posture and breathing habits and how this can lead to voice improvements.

Get it checked out by a doctor

If you experience difficulties with voice control or air supply to the vocal chords then there may be an underlying medical condition. If the cause of the difficulties is not known, then it is definitely worth having the condition checked out by a doctor. If you find that the problem is physical in nature, such as asthma, then appropriate medical intervention should be set in place.

I am a strong believer in using whatever resources are available, be they conventional medicine or a new age alternative. It is up to the individual to decide which balance is right for them between the various treatment approaches.

This open mindedness is part of the holistic philosophy.

PSYCHOLOGICAL CONDITIONS

Psychological influences can be many and varies. Often these psychological influences are subtle and express themselves in the form of physical symptoms.

The elective mute

Recently, I read an article in the local paper (Lawrence 1998) that illustrated the extremes that the body-mind can go to in order to stop us from vocalizing. The article told of a boy, Nick who had been an elective mute from kindergarten age to 10 years. The article told of his long recovery with the help of social workers and psychologists. Nick's recovery involved both patience and time consuming therapy.

The article quoted Nick as saying that, at a young age; "I just started not talking to anyone and I just continued – I don't know why. I just decided not to talk".

Mutism is one of the more extreme impairments of vocal production. Mutism has many causes and many forms. It can present as:–

- The inability to produce any sound at all.
- The inability to speak (aphasia).
- A reduced use of speech (dysphasia).

In Nick's case, the underlying cause was psychological. But, in other cases the cause may be primarily physical. Brain damage to certain areas can cause aphasia or dysphasia. Brain damage to other areas of the brain can cause impairment in the ability to hear or reproduce musical sounds.

In September 1998, I saw the beautiful Australian film called "Amy". It was about a young girl who was elective (or functional) deaf and mute. For those of you who have not seen the film, I won't spoil the plot. It is enough to say that Amy's condition was caused by a trauma.

She was not able to hear spoken works or to speak, but she could hear words that were sung and she could sing. Her recovery of normal speech and hearing functions involved a psychologist helping her to come to terms with the trauma.

Contributions to voice problems. Stress and lifestyle.

One of the clues to a voice problem having underlying psychological causes, is that the problem gets worse at times of psychological stress. Voice production seems to be particularly sensitive to stress in many people.

Many psychological and lifestyle factors can contribute to the quality of our speaking or singing voice. Stress and anxiety are obvious factors that can have a detrimental influence on the voice.

Our body, of course is the instrument that produces the voice. We need to look after our body in the following ways:–

1. By choosing a healthy life style.
2. Attempting to reduce the stress levels in our life.
3. Dealing with any underlying psychological issues that may be causing problems.

In chapter 7, I will talk about how to improve the way that we look after our bodies.

Stored physical and psychological trauma.
Memory in the muscles.

Voice problems can be caused by muscles not working properly because they carry the "memory" of past traumas. This is known as "memory in the muscles". Even when a physical injury is fully repaired, the muscles of our body can still carry memories of the trauma that caused the injury.

When muscles store traumatic memories, these muscles will not operate in a free and flexible way. These muscles are "on guard" and are "afraid" to work properly. If the muscles that still carry these "memories" of trauma are in the neck and throat, this can interfere with vocal production.

Muscles can carry memories of trauma even if that trauma was not physical in nature. For example, if a child spoke out and told the truth (as the child knew it) and there were traumatic consequences, the child could develop a fear of speaking out. This fear can take the form of tension in the throat and vocal chords. In its most dramatic form the fear could lead to elective mutism. This may have been a contributing cause of Nick's mutism.

I will deal with memory in the muscles in more detail in chapter 6.

Performance anxiety

When we can't get our voice to work properly at a time when we really need to, it is often due to performance anxiety. There appear to be two common situations where this anxiety occurs:

1. The first situation is the fear of "saying the wrong thing", particularly in relation to the spoken word.
2. The second situation is where the quality of one's voice is going to be judged. This is usually in relation to singing.

Performance anxiety can lead to a wide range of symptoms both physical and psychological. These include:–
- Cramping of the muscles used in voice production.
- Dryness of the throat.
- Shortage of breath due to shallow breathing, and poor breath control.
- Excessive perspiration.
- Temporary blanking of memory.
- Shaking and excessive tremor.
- Freezing in the sense of not being able to move, or having restricted movement.
- Nausea and butterflies in the stomach.

The fear of and form of vocal expression may range from very mild to extreme.

Mild fear

In its mild form, the fear of speaking or singing in public may be about feeling a bit awkward or mildly embarrassed.

Moderate fear

In a moderate form, a person may feel embarrassment, and even guilt and shame. He may feel tense and dry in the throat and feel "choked up".

Severe fear

With severe performance anxiety, a person is so terrified of any public exposure that they are totally incapable of performing.

Reasons for the anxiety: Secondary gains

Fear of singing may be represented in physical and psychological ways. However, the problems are manifested, we need to understand how the underlying psychological processes work in order to help with recovery. Our conscious mind does not want to feel scared of singing. Consciously, we want to enjoy singing and feel confident about it.

However, some subconscious system keeps the fear in place. That subconscious system believes that it is better to have the problem than fix it. In other words, it is dangerous not to feel anxious. This is called a secondary gain. The secondary gain is the pay off for staying in the dysfunctional state. Take the example of Nervous Nigel.

Case study:– Nervous Nigel

Nigel was a part time professional singer. He regularly developed laryngitis just before a big show. A powerful subconscious part of him did not want him to sing on the night.

Nigel was not even aware that this part didn't want him to sing on the night. Nevertheless, that powerful part had its way and the laryngitis got him out of singing on some occasions.

The secondary gain was his not singing on those occasions.

Medical and psychological treatment

If an underlying medical reason for your voice problem is found and you seek appropriate medical treatment, this should not rule out the need for psychological treatment as well. With a holistic approach, physical and psychological treatment strategies should be used to compliment each other.

One of the tragedies of main stream modern medicine is the lack of recognition of a holistic approach to healing. Most doctors that I have come across are reluctant to use psychotherapy as an adjunct in the treatment of conditions such as psoriasis (a type of skin disease) and endometriosis (adhesions in the abdominal cavity).

Many, if not most physical conditions that effect the voice, seem to be caused by a combination of both physical (medical) and psychological factors. As one example, an asthma attack can be brought on by stress in some people. The sufferer may be reacting to dust mites in the air (physical factor), but the reaction is more severe because the person feels stressed out (psychological factor).

I believe that most, if not all conditions which appear to be only physical in nature can benefit from psychological intervention in addition to any appropriate physical treatment. By the same token, psychological conditions can also benefit from body work. More about body work later.

Extreme views in the search for simple causes:

When an expert clinician assesses a condition such as asthma, they will make some estimation of the relative contribution of physical and psychological factors to the condition. The relative contribution will depend, in part on the belief system of the clinician.

The interaction of the psychological and the physical have always been of fascination to those in the healing profession. There are extreme views held at either end of the spectrum. At one end, there are those with the conservative view that psychological factors play little or no part in medical conditions.

At the other end are those who believe that all diseases are a matter of subconscious choice. In the case of cancer, they say that we chose to get it, therefore we can choose to heal it.

"It is all in the body" extreme

The doctor who treated Nigel believed that his condition was physical. The doctor tried all sorts of antibiotics, gargles, and dietary changes, but all to no avail, because the problem wasn't caused by a disease. It was only when Nigel went for treatment with a psychologist and dealt with his underlying anxiety about singing, that he began to recover from pre-performance laryngitis.

"It is all in the mind" extreme

Jim, who is a friend of mine, was effected by the "It is all in the mind" extreme view. Jim developed cancer of the liver. A therapist told Jim that he had chosen to give himself cancer and he could choose to cure the cancer. Although the therapist was well meaning, it turned out to be a damaging thing to say, because it just added guilt to Jim's list of problems. Jim began to believe that he had deliberately caused his own cancer and this caused him great distress.

Jim needed emotional support with a condition that had both physical and psychological components. Fortunately he did get that support from other sources.

The holistic middle ground

Both of these extreme views are harmful to the healing process. I believe that a holistic approach is best, where both physical (medical, physiotherapy etc) interventions and psychological interventions (psychotherapy, therapeutic body work etc) are used in combination.

There is an overwhelming body of evidence to support the view that the course of many illnesses can be influenced by changes in mental attitude. Interventions such as stress management and anxiety reduction have a good track record in assisting with the healing process.

CHAPTER 3

The Inner Critic and Performance

We carry around our own internal negative judge. We can't get rid of that judge, but we can change the way it works.

Poor techniques and negative judgements

Most people who come to me wanting to learn how to develop vocal strength and sing more confidently, have a combination of poor singing technique and a fear of having their singing voice judged by others. I will discuss how to improve singing techniques in a later chapter, but for now let us look in more detail at the parts that maintain the fear of singing.

By the time a person has come to a voice worker for help with their singing or spoken voice, their adult part has made the decision that the fears that they have of singing are unreasonable or exaggerated and they want to overcome these fears.

The "Inner Critic" & the "Frightened Child"

Most people that I see have at least two subconscious parts that contribute to a fear of singing. The first part can be called the "inner critic" and this part is responsible for making negative judgements about the quality of their voice.

The second part can be called the "frightened child". This part has learned that it is dangerous to take risks and believes that bad things are going to happen if they were to sing in front of other people.

The inner critic makes harsh judgements about our voice and the frightened child worries about how others will judge our voice. The inner critic and the frightened child have much in common and they can operate as a subconscious team to undermine our confidence in our singing ability.

For both these parts, it is fear that runs the show. It is fear that drives these parts to override our conscious decision to sing with confidence. Both of these parts are trying to protect us in the only ways that they know how.

Voice dialogue and selves

The "inner critic" is a concept developed by Hal and Sidra Stone (Stone 1993) as part of their "Voice Dialogue" theoretical framework. With voice dialogue, Hal and Sidra have presented the idea that we are made up of many parts called selves. (I will use the terms "self" and "part" interchangeably). These selves are subconscious psychological subsystems that play a role in how we think and behave. The inner critic is one such self. The number of other possible selves is limited only by the imagination. I refer to the "frightened child" as one such self.

The aware adult

With all these subconscious selves doing their own thing, who is meant to be running the show I hear you ask? The answer is an adult part of us is meant to be running the show. The adult part is the conscious part of us, of which we are fully aware, whose purpose is to oversee operations. Unlike the disowned selves, this part is fully known to us. The adult part can "stand back" from a situation and make an objective assessment of what is going on. This is our "rational part".

Hal and Sidra Stone refer to the adult part as the "aware ego". I prefer to call it, the "aware adult". When we have an unreasonable over-riding fear or we have some compulsive behaviour, then we know that the adult cannot be in charge.

Much of the therapy that I do is helping people get their adult back in charge of their life.

How much do you need to know about change?

When I work in the voice dialogue method, I am focussed on change and understanding of how a person operates. A dialogue is set up between subconscious part or parts and the aware adult. With this method the client usually understands how change is occurring because his aware adult is always involved. When a unit of voice dialogue work is completed, the information from this work is normally processed so that the client can understand what went on.

However, with other forms of therapy, change can occur without the need for conscious awareness or understanding by the client. With hypnosis in general, and Ericksonian hypnosis in particular, the client does not have to be aware of how changes occur (Haley 1993). Milton Erickson used a variety of techniques such as double binds, paradoxes and metaphors to confuse the conscious mind. The purpose of this was to overload the conscious mind and make it more likely that unconscious processes could take place without the over control of the conscious mind.

I have a personal preference for using techniques that leave the client with an understanding of what went on, but I realize that change without understanding is just fine.

The inner critic and standards

The inner critic is a part of us responsible for maintaining standards. It may have other roles as well. The inner critic has a lot of things to say about what we do and think, and all of them are critical and negatively judgmental. It is impossible to have good self esteem when you have a very powerful and active inner critic. In most of us, the inner critic has particularly harsh criticism reserved for when we sing.

"I don't want to say anything to encourage his inner critic."

In the first chapter I explained my theory that modern society had resulted in higher standards being set for vocal performance because of our greater exposure to high quality voices. The overactive inner critic has learned these higher standards and applies them with enthusiasm.

When we really listen to the inner critic, we may hear the voice of our critical mother, father, grand mother or whoever it was who said all those negative things about us when we were growing up.

The frightened child and consequences

The frightened child is afraid of the same sort of consequences as the inner critic, but operates differently. Whereas the inner critic will say things about how pathetic you are, the frightened child will say things about how dangerous or risky things are. The frightened child is afraid of the consequences of your actions in terms of how people will judge your actions.

When you listen to the frightened child, you may hear your own voice from a much earlier age.

Powerful covert operations

If a subconscious part has no power, it will have no say in running your life. It is only the powerful parts that have an influence. Psychological problems occur when a subconscious part has the power to overrule our adult decisions and does so. It is then that we may start to become aware of a subconscious part. These parts lead us to have thoughts we don't want to have (obsessional thoughts) and to engage in behaviours that we don't want to do (compulsive behaviours).

Some of our subconscious parts run benign operations. That is where there is no conflict between the aware adult and the subconscious part. It is only those parts that are in conflict with our adult that cause us trouble.

Quite often we have no awareness that these parts are there, determining our behaviour. For instance, we might know that we are frightened of singing, but we have no idea of what the fear is about and how it may have come into existence.

I have met people who believe that all their decisions are made by their conscious adult part. They are kidding themselves. I have never met a person for whom there isn't some behaviour controlled at a subconscious level.

Disowned selves

In the voice dialogue system, behaviour or beliefs that don't fit our image of ourselves are said to be disowned. These behaviour or beliefs are run by "disowned selves". A disowned self causes us distress because we don't believe that it is part of us. We say things like: "I'm not like that!" "I don't know what came over me". "I'm a really gentle and peace loving person, I would never say a thing like that". Etcetera, etcetera.

More often than not, a disowned part is suppressed and operates only at a non aware level. As a general rule, the more we try to disown a part, the more powerful it becomes.

Case study:– Gentle John

John has a disowned part that is responsible for his feelings of anger. John sees himself as a peace loving and friendly man who avoids conflict. He denies that he has any anger and is not aware of any angry feelings. This means that his anger is suppressed and run by a disowned self.

John doesn't even know when he is feeling angry. It comes through in the form of sarcastic comments and passive aggression. John has throat problems. He has a soft weak voice and he has to continually keep clearing his throat when he is speaking. John's throat problems are caused by his denial of his anger.

Deep inside, he might really want to yell out in anger, but he suppresses this urge and speaks in a controlled and soft voice.

Because John disowns his anger and doesn't want to know about it, he can never learn to really have control over it. He can only suppress it and the anger comes out in different forms.

But in some people, the inner critic is disowned. It is much easier to deal with our inner critic when we can hear what it is saying. It is much more difficult if it is disowned, and we are not even aware of it operating. In chapter 4, I will discuss how we can learn to better hear what subconscious parts are saying.

Case study:– Owned Owen

Owen is a person with a reasonable level of self awareness. He knows about his singing inner critic, and he owns his inner critic. A conversation that I had with him went as follows:–

Owen: "I know I give myself a hard time when I sing."

Dick: "How do you know that?"

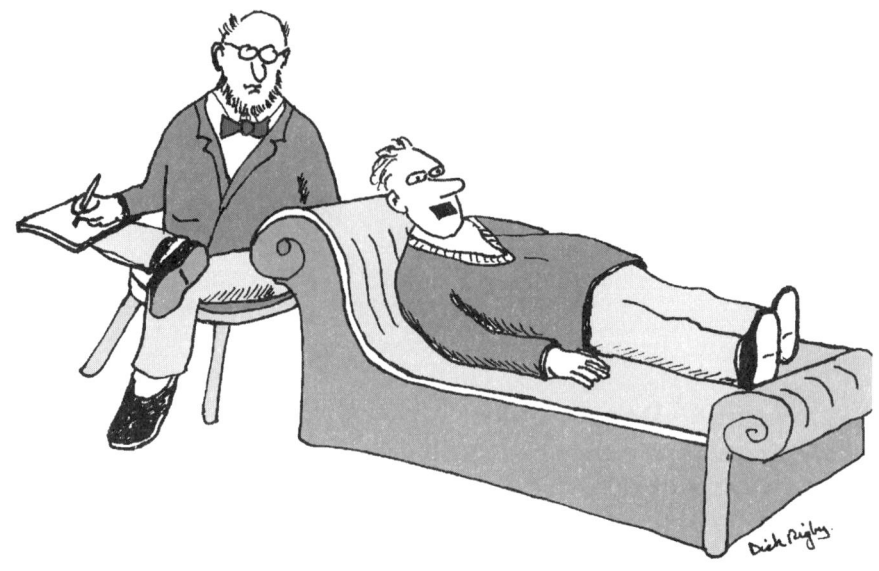

"My Inner Critic doesn't understand me"

Owen: "I can hear a voice inside say really critical things about my voice."
Dick: "Are those things that it says true?"
Owen: "I think that this voice makes it sound much worse than it really is".

Owen's understanding that his inner critic exaggerates, is the first stage in his recovery from his fears.

Case study:– Disowned Denise

Denise is a person with a low level of self awareness. She disowns her inner critic. A recent conversation that I had with her went as follows:–

Denise: "I have a really lousy singing voice".
Dick: "How do you know that?"
Denise: "Well you've only got to listen to me to hear that I have".
Dick: "You sound ok to me".
Denise: "But of course you are going to say that because you are my therapist".
Dick: "But how do you really know your voice is lousy?"
Denise: "Because I can hear that it is lousy".

This type of conversation will be familiar to many of you with its quality of going round in circles. We hear the influence of her hidden inner critic. Denise is not aware that it is a part of her that holds a particular view point and that her adult part could hold a different viewpoint from the inner critic. Her inner critic is in a very powerful position because it can not be challenged without apparently challenging what Denise the adult believes to be true.

In therapy, I would work with helping her to understand that her inner critic is only a part of her and that her aware adult can hold a different point of view. I would encourage her to see her inner critic as a separate part who happens to hold a different view from that of the adult and to get her to develop a dialogue with her inner critic.

But what if what Denise says is right and she does have a lousy voice?

Well, even lousy voices can be improved. When she came to see me, her inner critic wouldn't ever give her a break and let her sing. So she never got a chance to learn how to improve her voice.

In some people the "inner critic speak" can be extremely harsh. We may hear the inner critic say "You have the worst singing voice in the world". "You are totally tone deaf". "You would be totally humiliated if you were to sing in public". "People are going to think you are a total drop kick". In her conscious mind, Denise is not aware that her inner critic keeps saying all these terrible things about her. She just felt bad about herself.

Absolute negatives become self defeating talk

The inner critic and the frightened child will usually make absolute statements of fact such as; "I have a really lousy singing voice"; or "I could never sing like that".

These absolute negative statements can become a self fulfilling prophesy. The statements leave no room for change or learning. In therapy I try and get people to change and take the "absolute" out of these statements:–

1. "I have a really lousy singing voice" – becomes; "My singing voice could do with improvement".
2. "I could never sing like that" – becomes; "I haven't learned to sing like that yet".

Case study:– Self Judging Janice

Janice came to see me with a desire to be more confident in her singing. She was not as self critical as Denise, but she said that her voice wasn't particularly good and if she were to sing in front of people she would feel humiliated. At home, she was able to sing and really enjoy her singing, but if either of her children or her husband were about, she would be criticized.

Her children would say, "Mum stop that horrible noise". Her husband would say, "Can I hear those cats fighting again"?

Her inner critic would then back up what her family had to say and tell herself that she had a terrible voice and she shouldn't impose it on other people. Actually, Janice has a very pleasant voice, but she could not fully enjoy her voice because of a combination of her inner critic and the external criticisms of her family.

Janice had learned her love of singing from her mother and her fear of judgement from her father. Janice's pattern had been learned from her family of origin. Her mother enjoyed singing and her father would be critical of her mother's singing. Janice wanted her mother to join a choir, but her mother didn't think that her voice was good enough.

The burden of perfectionism
Case study:– Perfect Patricia

Patricia's background was different from Janice. Her mother was a singing teacher. Patricia learned from her mother to strive for perfection and the enjoyment of singing was not particularly important. Patricia's mother hoped that Patricia would go on to be the opera singer that Patricia's mother never was. Patricia's mother always wanted to be an opera singer, but was never given the opportunity or the encouragement by her parents to do this.

Patricia's mum tried to fulfill her own life's ambition through her daughter. Hence Patricia grew up with an overly developed inner critic always striving for perfection and she could never be satisfied until perfection was achieved.

Of course this meant that she could never be satisfied because perfection cannot be achieved. The joy of singing didn't even come into it.

Perfectionists can never win

It seems to me that having an overactive inner critic can have two outcomes. It can result in a person becoming a perfectionist, or it can make a person just give up and stop trying. Or a person may alternate between the two extremes. Perfectionists strive to "get it just right". They can never be really happy with anything that they create because their creations always fall short of their perfect standard.

Usually perfectionists will try and avoid doing tasks in the areas where their inner critic is strongest. If your inner critic holds strong views about singing, then you will probably try and avoid singing.

With the help of alcohol

One way to beat the perfectionism bug is with alcohol. Nearly every alcoholic that I have ever treated has been a perfectionist. Drinking alcohol gets rid of the inner critic while the alcohol is in the system. A person who could not possibly sing in public while in a sober state will sing quite confidently when they are drunk. I suspect that many people who perform in karioke bars are well lubricated before they do so.

Much of my work with alcoholics is concerned with reducing the negative influence of the inner critic so that they can learn to do in a sober state what they could previously only do when they are drunk. I see alcohol as a "drug of permission". By drinking to get rid of the inner critic, it gives the drinker permission to do things he could not do when he was sober.

The system works so well that alcoholics are very reluctant to change. However, as any one who has had to live with an alcoholic knows, alcoholism has its many down sides. Among these are:–

1. Along with the loss of the inner critic goes the loss of judgement and discrimination.
2. The "day after" the inner critic usually gets stuck in with redoubled enthusiasm. That is if the drunk remembers what he did.
3. The alcoholic never learns anything because any lessons learned in the drunk state do not transfer to the sober state or visa versa.

A similar picture applies with other addictions.

When I work with rehabilitating alcoholics, I will use voice dialogue to help reduce the impact of the inner critic thereby reducing the need to get drunk.

Good and bad inner critics

All of this inner critic bashing give the impression that the inner critic is all "bad news". Not so. The inner critic is essential to monitoring what we do. I have treated people whose inner critic was underdeveloped. Take the case of Cathy.

Case study:– Confident Cathy

Cathy has low inhibition and consequently is impulsive in her actions. She has an inflated opinion of her abilities and her singing in particular. Even if she sang out of tune, that wouldn't prevent her from singing in public. Cathy has an underdeveloped inner critic. She does not fully evaluate her actions and just acts on impulse. If what she does has a bad outcome she says to herself "what the hell", or "that wasn't my fault". It is like she is in a drunken state without drinking.

At one stage, Cathy was diagnosed as having "Attention Deficit Hyperactive Disorder". Needless to say, Cathy gets into a lot of hot water. There are secondary gains for Cathy being this way in that her mother always rescues her. But that's another story.

It is to Cathy's advantage to strengthen the role of her inner critic so that she can be less impulsive, more considered in her judgements enabling her to evaluate her behaviour more realistically after an incident.

The developing inner critic

The inner critic learns its role mostly during childhood. This was illustrated in chapter 1. Judgmental and critical parents will tend to develop strong inner critics in their children.

Cathy grew up in a household where she was not criticized. Her parents were permissive and indulgent to the point of being dysfunctional. She received a lot of praise as a child and she continued to test her parents' boundaries with more and more outrageous behaviour. Usually, she would have boundaries placed on her only after she had engaged in some extreme behaviour. These boundaries were seldom enforced over time. More often than not, she would be rescued and others blamed for the consequences of her behaviour.

Cathy never had good enough boundaries set on her to enable her to develop a healthy inner critic.

Perfect Patricia was the opposite. I mentioned Patricia earlier. She was the one with the opera singer mother who caused Patricia to develop an overactive inner critic. Her mother was critical and strove for perfection. Patricia was trained this way from the moment she began to talk. She internalized her mothers critical statements which began to form the repertoire of her inner critic.

But this was not enough for Patricia. Patricia really wanted to please her mother and gain acceptance, so Patricia's inner critic made her internal statements even stronger than those of her mother. The inner critic reasoned that if she set standards even higher than her mother's, this would further increase her chances of pleasing her mother or at least reducing the risk of exposure to mum's harsh criticisms

This was Patricia's subconscious way of gaining control over the situation. By making its own harsh judgements, the inner critic could get in before mum.

When selves develop their own identities at an early age and split off from the adult to become disowned selves, they often have a child's way of looking at the world. In the therapy work that I do, I prefer to call such a part an "inner child" rather than a "disowned self".

In this sense the inner critic can also be seen as an inner child because it is not able to properly update information in the current world.

Patricia was able to attend a small supportive singing therapy group. She began to tune into her voices of her various parts including her inner critic. She reported that one day in her singing group she had the following internal dialogue:–

Aware adult: "It is fine for me to sing here. I am among friends and my mother is a thousand kilometers away. I am as safe as I could be".

Inner critic: "You are not safe to sing here. Somehow your mother will find out. Anyway these people are only pretending to be accepting of you. Really, behind your back they are treating you as a laughing stock".

The inner critic and the frightened child are colluding. The frightened child is frightened that something bad is going to happen if Patricia sings, ie her mother will find out. This part is so frightened that it will not allow her aware adult part to look at the situation objectively. The frightened child invents a fantasy to support her belief that Patricia is not safe.

The inner critic colludes with this fantasy and says that she has a terrible voice.

Every part is trying to do the right thing

Bandler and Grinder developed Neurolinguistic Programming in the 1970's (Bandler & Grinder 1979). I believe that one of the most important statements of principle that they made was, that every part of us is trying to look after us in some way. This principle has been a central plank to my therapy ever since I learned about it. There are no "devils" inside us that have to be exorcised. There are just parts that have different ideas from our aware adult about how to look after us.

There may be wars going on inside and many a headache has been caused by such wars. These headaches are just caused by different parts fighting over the best thing to do.

The inner supporter

To counteract the inner critic we need an inner supporter. It is the inner supporter's role to comfort and reassure. The inner supporter

Tug of war

may be some part that was developed in childhood or it may be a part that we have to develop in our adult life.

Some children grow up in families with virtually no emotional support. In these families, there is no model for these children to learn about emotional support. The aware adult has to learn how to look after and support the inner children from scratch.

Where there is no model within the family, children may look outside the family for appropriate role models. Such learning would not only have to rely on what these children learn from watching functional models, but would also rely in part on their genetically programed knowledge of parenting.

The inner critic and voice

An overactive inner critic can have a number of different effects on the voice:–

1. I won't sing at all.

The first, and most obvious effect is that a person just doesn't sing at all. In the most extreme form a person won't even sing in private because they can't stand the sound of their own voice. Or at least the inner critic can't stand the sound. This is a very sad situation.

2. I can't sing in public.

The person who can't sing in front of other people accounts for a significant proportion of people with inhibitions about singing. This is a form of performance anxiety. The inner critic will allow him to sing in private and even to enjoy singing in the shower, but the thought of other people's judgements on the quality of his singing is terrifying.

3. I get stage fright.

The individual is able to sing in front of other people and even believes that his voice will sound ok. But when he starts to sing, he experiences levels of anxiety and he is not able to produce the quality of note that he was able to produce in the shower. For such individuals, the hidden frightened child part takes over and jams the system up when he attempts to perform.

Even experienced professional singers can suffer from voice production problems due to anxiety. I believe that is why many professional singers turn to alcohol or some related drug, to sedate the anxiety.

The inner critic's effect on the body

The messages that the inner critic sends will have an effect on the neuromuscular system of the body. The effect is usually an increase in the tension of muscles. The increased muscle tension results in reduced control over the operation of these muscles or groups of muscles.

Those groups of muscles which will have a direct effect on singing include throat muscles (in particular those controlling the voice box), neck muscles, the diaphragm, and the inter costal (rib cage) muscles. The longitudinal muscles of the back and other muscles controlling posture also have an effect on voice production by effecting the pattern of breathing.

How to change the inner critic

In the next chapter I will deal with how to heal the voice that is in trouble. I will discuss ways of changing the way that the inner critic and the frightened child operate, and reducing the sometimes crippling influence of the inner critic.

These changes can lead to:–

1. Reducing the fear of singing, ie developing more confidence in singing and speaking.
2. Reducing muscular tension leading to more flexibility and control over breathing and voice production.

CHAPTER 4

Healing the Voice

Healing the voice is like walking through a
doorway into a new world .

Healing the voice versus healing with the voice

As we know, the voice-body is an instrument capable of doing many wondrous things. In chapter 9, I will talk more about how the voice can be used as an instrument of healing. But before the voice can be used to heal, it has to be in proper working order.

In the first chapter we learned how childhood experiences can shape our fears and reduce our confidence in our singing voice. I discussed how the inner critic and the frightened child can be set up.

When the inner critic is overactive, a person can never be confident with their singing voice and cannot enjoy singing. Also, when the "frightened child" is too frightened to be negotiated with, this part can turn the singing experience into a phobia and ruin an experience that should otherwise be enjoyable.

This chapter deals with the many ways of changing the parts that cripple the expression of our voice.

> ***I am adamant when I say that people who are afraid to sing can learn to sing confidently.***

Basic principles of therapy.

There are certain basic beliefs that I follow when working with powerful subconscious parts in order to heal and strengthen the voice.

These principles are:–

1. All parts are trying to do the right thing to look after us and keep us out of danger. A part that is disowned or denied will have a very different way of looking at the world than our aware

adult and this part may need to be changed and updated in order for us to function more effectively. It is important to note that not all the beliefs held by subconscious parts are wrong or out of date.

2. There can be great wisdom held by our subconscious parts and sometimes what our conscious mind wants may not be the best thing for us. Just as we can teach our subconscious parts how to be in the present, we have much to learn from the knowledge held by these subconscious parts. Maybe this subconscious knowledge is what some people call intuition.

3. That no subconscious part can be removed from you. As much as we would like to banish those parts that stop us doing what we want to do, those parts are here to stay. So we had better get used to the idea of working with them.

4. Therapy involves learning that these subconscious parts exist and about the role that they play.

5. Therapy involves learning about how to negotiate between the aware adult and these various parts. Through this process, we make the journey towards integration and recovery.

6. Central to recovery, is the intention to accept and nurture all parts. Nurturing does not mean indulgence. There are occasions where strong boundaries need to be set on a subconscious part. Nurturing and boundaries are essential to change. Just beating up on these subconscious parts does not produce the change we want and usually makes the dysfunctional parts more hidden and more powerful.

7. The style of therapy that a therapist uses should fit the client rather than visa versa.

For people with a fear of singing or vocal expression of any kind, learning how to nurture these parts is essential to learning how to nurture the voice.

Compulsive behaviours, addictive behaviours and singing phobias

At various points in this book I refer to addictive and compulsive behaviours and to phobias. I think of compulsive, addictive and phobic behaviours as much the same thing. Phobias are just compulsive fears.

In this sense, a compulsive behaviour is any behaviour that is run by a subconscious part that is in conflict with the aware adult, and the aware adult cannot control the thoughts or actions of that subconscious part. For some people, their fear of singing is a compulsive behaviour. As an adult, they want to sing, but a subconscious part stops them.

In the past, the term addictive behaviour has been applied mainly to alcohol and drugs. I believe that the models that have been developed for the treatment of substance addictions are just as applicable for the treatment of other addictions such as compulsive gambling, sex addiction, personal danger addiction, compulsive spending, work or study addiction, food addiction and weight addiction. The list goes on.

Avoidance of singing or speaking due to unreasonable fear is just another example of addiction. The avoidance is the addictive behaviour. By a person withdrawing from singing when they really want to sing, they reduce their anxiety and avoid dealing with underlying issues.

Further on in the book, I have described a form of addiction that I have called "esoteric addiction". This is where a person uses contact with mystical and other experiences in an addictive way.

"Compulsive, addictive behaviours are not about being hungry, thirsty, horny or needing to work. They are about mood alteration. They help us manage our own feelings. They distract us or alter the way we are feeling so we don't have to feel the loneliness and emptiness of our abandonment and shame".

Bradshaw (1998)

Case study:– Phobic Peter

Peter wanted to sing in front of a group of close friends. His aware adult knew that it would be quite safe for him to do so. His adult knew that his friends would not ridicule him and would appreciate his singing. However, Peter had an overwhelming terror that prevented him from singing. His fear was so strong and so out of touch with reality that it could be described as a phobia.

Peter came into therapy asking for help with his phobia of singing. He asked his therapist for help in controlling or overcoming this behaviour. His therapist was able to help Peter diminish the intensity of this compulsive fear of singing.

Sometimes one can get lucky, and therapy can produce a permanent cure of a phobia.

TYPES OF THERAPY

There are many different therapeutic approaches, techniques and styles that are effective in strengthening confidence and the power of the voice. The therapy that I use involves using a mix of different techniques and philosophies. The so called eclectic approach. In this chapter, I will discuss those techniques that I have found to be the most useful.

A. SKELETONS FROM THE PAST: REGRESSIVE THERAPY

In order for some people to recover confidence in their voice, it is necessary for them to learn something about how they lost their confidence in the first place. This is so they can make sense of why it is the way it is. For other people, it is not necessary or relevant to delve into the past, but just to work with the present and the future.

Most therapy that I do is a balance between the two. The right mix between past and present will depend on the person and their background.

One clue to the need to do regressive therapy work is, when a person has no idea of how their voice problems developed because their childhood was "just wonderful", and there is no obvious physical explanation for the problems. Here, the person is probably in denial. If everything was so wonderful, how did the voice problems develop in the first place?

> *"Any treatment of a child that is less*
> *than nurturing is abusive to a child".*
> Mellody (1992).

Most children who have grown up in dysfunctional families need to create some form of idealization of their family in order to cope with the distress of the dysfunction. Some adult clients of mine have presented with an idealization of their childhood whereas, in fact, their childhood was quite awful. Henry's case illustrates this well.

Case study:– Regarding Henry

Henry came to me saying that he had problems with self confidence in general and with his speaking voice in particular. As a trainer of sales personnel, his work required that he present seminars every now and then. For several days before he was due to present an important seminar, Henry was in turmoil. He couldn't sleep properly at night, he was anxious and irritable and his family found him "a pain to live with".

It was clear to me that he was a very anxious man and that his voice problems appeared to be anxiety related.

In his first session with me, I asked him how he got to be this way? He said that he didn't know because he had a really good childhood and a loving family. By the second session he had volunteered some information that made more sense of it. His father had been an alcoholic who was regularly physically and verbally violent to him and to his mother.

Within the family the father's drinking was denied and never spoken about. Everyone pretended that it was a wonderful family.

Even after Henry admitted the violence, he played it down. He said; "Life was pretty good apart from the beatings". His mother was a very meek and timid woman who wanted to keep the peace at all costs and would never stand up in support of Henry against his father. A true codependent. The mother would say "Don't do anything to upset your father, you know what he's like when he gets angry".

How could a child's self confidence develop in such a damaged household. He related one particularly traumatic incident that left a permanent imprint on Henry's mind. In grade 8 he had come home from school with an "A" for an essay that he had composed and read to the class. His drunken father insisted that Henry read it to him. The father ridiculed and poured scorn on the essay. As a consequence the father demolished Henry's self confidence in public speaking.

This was one of many similar incidences, but this one in particular stood out in Henry's mind.

Healing Henry

Therapy with Henry involved several stages:–

1. Firstly we had to look at his family for what it really was and not what he had made it in his imagination. It took many sessions for Henry to learn that his family had not been wonderful. This acceptance involved Henry grieving for a lost childhood.
2. Secondly it was necessary for Henry to connect with the feelings that he had concerning relevant traumatic memories such as the one of his father humiliating his English essay.

3. The final stage was to assist him in recovery from the trauma so that he could regain confidence in his voice.

For Henry, it was necessary for him to come to terms with the past in order for him to recover his confidence in his voice.

B. EMOTIONAL RELEASE WORK WITH THE VOICE

Getting the mix right

Just as the right mix is important between the present and the past, it is equally important to get the right mix between emotional release and cognitive understanding.

Some therapists work mainly in the style of cognitive behavioural therapy. With this style, there is an emphasis placed on thinking (cognitive) processes and little emphasis placed on emotional expression or emotional release (catharsis).

Some therapists work at the other end of the scale with "dynamic" techniques such as psychodrama, gestalt, rebirthing, and primal therapy. With these emotion based therapies, people are encouraged to express and release emotions.

I believe that the best therapy is done by balancing the cognitive and emotional aspects. Many people need guidance in therapy in order to get the balance right. People who are "in their head" all the time need some guidance to get in touch with their emotions. People who are overly emotional, benefit from guidance to set up a cognitive structure with boundaries to make sense of what they are dealing with and where they are heading.

Working with emotions

With almost any form of therapy strong emotions will come up. The regressive therapy done with Henry, brought strong feelings to the surface. Emotions that had been locked away for many years started to surface. Such strong emotions of traumatic memories have to be dealt with in a skilled, loving and understanding way.

It concerns me when I hear of people who have had strong emotions brought to the surface, and these feelings have not been properly dealt with. For most people, it is relatively easy to bring strong feelings to the surface using "dynamic" techniques.

The far more difficult part is to make sure that the emotions are resolved in a healthy way. If traumatic emotions are brought to the surface and not dealt with properly, the person can be worse off. In a sense, the trauma is reinforced.

Using the voice to release emotions

One way of bringing strong emotions to the surface is by helping a person develop greater power in the expression of his voice. For example, a person who has never sung loudly in his life, will experience strong emotions the first time he learns to sing loudly.

Another example of the release of strong feelings is the emotional buzz a person can feel when he sings in front of others for the first time with confidence. The feelings felt here may be that of empowerment and exhilaration.

However, some strong feelings that come up may be more difficult to deal with. The feelings may be fear or anger. It takes skill and understanding for a therapist to effectively deal with these strong feelings when they come up. The therapist must be careful, caring, accepting and patient to allow a person to work through these feelings.

> *"Emotions are the power house*
> *where voice and singing are*
> *concerned and breath is the vehicle."*

Henry connected with his strong feelings of grief, sadness, anger and fear concerning the memories of his childhood. When this happened, he needed a good deal of support and reassurance as he came to terms with his childhood. Many people, particularly men like Henry, feel disconnected from their emotions at the beginning of therapy.

There are many ways of helping disconnected people get in touch. Generally, I favour gentle methods, particularly where the voice is involved.

Emotions are the power house where voice and singing are concerned.

When Henry became aware of a strong feeling connected with his childhood, I encouraged him to stay with this feeling and use his breath to help him stay connected. This process allowed him to reach a point of deep sadness essential for him to accept, to heal and to recover.

Empowerment through healing voice work

Empowering the voice is about teaching a person to form a deep connection with their personal power. Some people lost the connection with their personal power when they were very young. They learned to be very frightened of expressing power through their voice.

They learned to be frightened of the consequences when they tried to express this power.

When a person comes into therapy wanting to develop greater power and confidence with their voice, one of the first things that a therapist should assess is the degree of safety that presently exists in the person's life. In the case of Henry, the dangers to his speaking out were now past and part of his childhood. These dangers were not present in his adult life. He had a supportive and understanding wife and a supportive work environment.

In other cases, it may not be safe for a person to speak out. In such cases, voice empowerment work has to be handled with care and sensitivity to the person's environment.

Yelling to heal

While the "gentle" approach to emotional release works in many situations, there are occasions where a good shout, yell or scream is

required to release an emotional bottle neck. For those who have lost the ability to use their voice loudly and powerfully, they need patient encouragement to rediscover the skill. Healing voice work encourages such people to develop the skills to speak loudly. When I work with such a person, I may help to build confidence by encouraging them to begin to use percussive sounds such as "Bah", said loudly over and over.

Some therapy centres have sufficient privacy to allow clients to shout, scream or yell out in safety. Some centres even provide a "screaming room" for this purpose.

If these facilities are not available in the therapy centre that you attend, and you need to yell and scream, there is another way. Take a drive in the country and yell at the bush or go to the beach to yell at the surf

If you try this, I recommend that you yell something which could not be heard by passers-by as a distress call. Sounds like "Bah" or "Yah" or "Woah" are relatively safe. A scream is not. "Cooee" is a good one for the Australian bush.

It is desirable when finishing off powerful expressive emotional release voice work to end with a soft sound. After a session of yelling at the surf, you should finish with several minutes of toning with a soft "oo", preferably followed by a period of 5 to 10 minutes silence. This soft sound is for grounding – to allow the body to return to a calmer, more grounded state.

Sometimes quite strong feelings are released by the shouting. These feelings might be feelings of energy and empowerment or feelings of sadness. Grounding and processing are important after emotionally intense work.

In a therapy session which involves emotional work, I like to end up with cognitive processing to help a person make sense of what they went through. It is not always possible to do the cognitive processing at the finish of an emotionally intense session. It may take a person several hours or even days to digest what has gone on.

However, as a general rule, some processing should take place in the next therapy session.

In overcoming blocks to expression, it is important that a person actually expresses the power of their voice, rather than just talking about expressing it.

To every thing, there is a season; a time to talk and a time to yell.

To every thing, there is a season and
A time to every purpose under heaven.
A time to be born, and a time to die,
A time to plant and a time to reap,
A time to kill and a time to heal,
A time to laugh and a time to weep.
Based on Ecclesiastes 3: 1-8

C. CORE PROFILING

"Core profiling" was co-developed by Nikki Nemerouf, and is well described in Roz Nutting's book (Nutting 1998). There are two states that we can be in. The first is the "Functional state" or "Authentic state", which is that of the rational adult. The second is the "Survival state" or "Coping state", which is that of the primitive fight or flight part of us. Certain events can trigger us into reacting in our survival state. Often these survival mechanisms are based on belief systems, called "Core beliefs", that were established in our childhood and are now well out of date.

But they are very resistant to change.

Nemerouf defines a trigger as; "A stimulus experienced as a real, imagined or anticipated loss of safety, love, well-being, control or positive regard". The trigger taps into a "core belief". It is this core belief that is stored deep in the subconscious that drives the dysfunctional coping behaviour. Core profiling is used in healing and involves the recognition, understanding and changing of dysfunctional core beliefs.

Roz Nutting points out that most of our core beliefs have been formed by the time we were seven or eight years old. Prior to this time a child's thought patterns are egocentric and magical. When a child, below the age of eight interprets a traumatic event it is likely to be interpreted in terms of this magical thinking.

For example; a six year old girl's father died suddenly from a heart attack. The father had been upset and yelled at his daughter the night before he died because she had not put her toys away as he had asked her to do.

Using egocentric and magical thinking, the child interprets the death as her fault. The core belief set up is; "If I hadn't been so naughty, my daddy wouldn't have been taken away".

The core belief set up by the egocentric and magical thinking was that:-

1. Her father's death was caused by her not putting her toys away that night.
2. His death was caused only by the single event with the toys.

This core belief could influence her actions for the rest of her life. When the girl becomes an adult, the core belief gets transferred from her father to any loved one in her life. She may live in constant fear of abandonment by her husband were she to say or do the wrong thing. She may become over protective of her children for fear that they suddenly will be taken away or be killed.

In my experience, most core beliefs have something to do with the fear of abandonment or rejection.

Case study:- Self Judging Janice

You will remember Janice from chapter 3. She was the one with a pleasant voice. But she had an overwhelming inner critic that prevented her from singing in front of other people, even her own family. Having to sing in front of other people triggered Janice's coping state. Her fear was that she would be humiliated. She believed that she was going to make a fool of herself in front of her friends and they would negatively judge her, and ridicule her.

Underpinning this was her core belief that she was not worthwhile and that her friends could not be trusted to support her if she tried to sing. This core belief was learned in her childhood interactions with her negative and judgmental father. The core belief was later reinforced by the criticisms of her husband and her own children.

Core profiling would help Janice identify her triggers and core beliefs. Through greater awareness at the time when her triggers were being activated, she would know better how to intervene to stop the primitive survival reaction.

D. INTERNAL DIALOGUE WORK

I mentioned in chapter 3 how voice dialogue is one very effective method for conducting inner negotiations to overcome fears. The wonderful thing about voice dialogue work is that it allows us to hear the selves that are within us as separate voices.

No longer does Phobic Peter say "I am afraid to sing in front of people". He learns to say that "There is a powerful part of me that is afraid to sing in front of people". "My aware adult has no major problems with singing in front of others". This separation of the parts is the beginning of Peter's recovery.

Talking to yourself is a sign of madness

You will be familiar with the popular saying that, "Talking to yourself is the first sign of madness". Well, nothing could be further from the truth. We all have internal voices. Learning how to separate the parts within us and begin to dialogue with these parts is the first stage of recovery.

The psychotic voices that schizophrenics hear are different in nature. These voices usually seem to come from an outside source. The sufferer may hear God or the devil giving instructions to him. During a psychotic episode, the sufferer can totally lose touch with reality. I believe that, in most cases, it is unwise to use voice dialogue to treat a psychotic person. However, in some cases of psychosis, there can be merit in using voice dialogue.

But for a non psychotic person, internal dialogue is a wonderful healing technique.

The aware adult

In chapter 3, I talked about the "aware adult" (or "aware ego"). This is the part that can stand back from a situation and make an objective assessment. It is this part that is put in charge of the negotiations with other parts. I also discussed the "inner critic" and the "frightened child".

I think that the best way to show how these parts can interact is by way of an example.

Case study:– Self Judging Janice again

As I mentioned before, Janice's singing voice had been criticized by her judgmental father and was now criticized by her children and her husband. As if that wasn't enough, she was given a hard time by her own inner critic.

In her third session with me she agreed to try some inner dialogue work. She related a particular incident when she was at a party and various people had sung songs to the accompaniment of a karioke machine. John, who was a friend of hers, asked Janice to sing a song of her choice. She freaked out and refused to sing, and felt embarrassed at not being able to join in with her friends.

I asked her what sorts of things went through her mind when she had been asked to sing. At first, she had some difficulty even hearing what her inner voices were saying. Our conversation went like this:–

Dick: "What did you say to yourself when John asked you to sing"?

Janice: " I don't know, I guess I said that my voice wouldn't sound good".

Dick: "What else did you hear this part saying"?

Janice: "I heard the part say, if you can't sing then don't bother trying".

It sounded to me like Janice was understating the strength of the self criticism. Most people do this. Her inner critic is still partly hidden. I helped Janice to listen to her voice more carefully.

Dick: "That sounds pretty mild. Would you listen again to this voice. This time more carefully. Don't edit what starts to come through. Just let me know exactly what it is that you hear this voice saying."

Janice: "Well actually, the part is saying that my singing voice is quite disgusting, nobody wants to hear it and it would be a totally humiliating experience for me to sing."

At this point, I could have continued by using either gestalt therapy or voice dialogue. With gestalt therapy I could have asked her who the critical voice reminded her of. She probably would have said that the critical part sounds like her father. I could have asked her to imagine putting her critical father on an empty chair and begun a dialogue with this critical father.

I preferred to use voice dialogue in this situation. Rather than to think of this part as her father, I asked her to think of it as her own inner critic. I asked Janice to imagine putting her inner critic out on the empty chair next to her.

At first she had some difficulty imagining this, but eventually she got some sense of having the inner critic out on the chair. Then I asked her to sit in that chair and become the inner critic. In making this move, she left the aware adult behind in the chair she had just vacated.

Dick: "So you are the part that is critical of Janice's singing voice".

Inner Critic: "Yes I am".

Dick: "How long have you been around?"

Inner Critic: "For ever".

Dick: "I guess that you have a tough job making sure that Janice doesn't make a fool of herself."
Inner Critic: "Yes it is tough. If I didn't stop her, she would make a total idiot of herself every day".
Dick: "And I guess nobody even thanks you for keeping the standards".
Inner Critic: "No".
Dick: "And who looks after you?"
Inner Critic: "I have to look after myself. I always have".
Dick: "That must get lonely at times."
Inner critic: "Yes it does."

At this point the inner critic starts to soften. I become aware of some sadness in the inner critic. Dialogue for change can begin. I asked Janice to return to the aware adult chair and begin to talk to her Inner critic. I suggested that she offer comfort to her inner critic. With each of the following interactions, she changed chairs.

Aware adult: "I understand that it is hard for you to be on guard all the time".
Inner critic: "It is, but if I didn't do it you would keep doing stupid things."

The Inner Critic

Aware adult: "Yes, but maybe if we talk more, I can be more careful of what I do. You could let me do things like singing when I feel it is safe."

Inner critic: "I don't know. — — — — Maybe I could".

This is the beginning of change.

The above example is a cut down version of what really happened. I have just described the essentials. Because of this, it gives the appearance that the process is simpler than it really was. In the real world, it can take some time for an effective dialogue to be set up.

But this example illustrates that a system that has been frozen for many years is beginning to loosen up.

The work continued with Janice over many sessions, coming back to this dialogue and continuing to reinforce that it should be the adult's call as to what is a potentially dangerous situation. It reached a resolution as Janice began to accept the inner critic as a part of her. She imagined hugging the inner critic to her chest and said, "Another part to have and to hold and to hug".

Gradually Janice developed more confidence in her singing, and she was able to ask her immediate family for their support. She explained to them how important it was for her to become confident in her singing and how important their support was to her.

The family agreed to be more supportive. They had some difficulties at first in not criticizing her singing, but mostly they got it right.

Since this time, Janice has learned to sing with confidence and not worry so much about what people will think of her.

The false adult

I have termed the phrase "False adult". This is the condition when we believe that what we are saying is coming from our "aware adult", but, in fact it is coming from the negative core belief systems of an inner child. The false adult sounds very reasonable and rational, just like an adult. But it is misleading.

How many times have you had a conversation with someone close to you and it sounds like they are making sense? But when you listen really carefully to what they are saying, it doesn't really make sense. Information is being used in a very selective way to support their case. They are in their false adult. If you challenge them, they will deny this and say that they are in their rational adult.

The "true adult" or "aware adult" operates on belief systems that are updated with current information about how the world works. The inner child operating on negative core beliefs takes in only information that support the negative core belief.

The true adult is objective and the false adult is selective.

The true adult is empathic, the false adult is egocentric.

All lies and jest,
still a man hears
what he wants to hear
and disregards the rest.
"The Boxer" Paul Simon 1968

The art of being functional is to know when you are in this state and to do something about getting the aware adult back in charge.

Separation of the voices

The effectiveness of the voice dialogue technique is the ability to separate the voices and begin a dialogue between the parts. It is the separation of the voices and the dialogue between them that facilitates the change.

Positive affirmations

Positive affirmations are one effective way of talking to yourself or your inner child, and building your self esteem. Affirmations can be really helpful. However, the misuse of positive affirmations in the past have tended to give them a bad name. For example, an affirmation can be potentially harmful if it:–

1. Is unrealistic.
2. Tells a lie.
3. Sets up an expectation which is too high.

Examples of the above are:–

1. *Unrealistic.* "I can do anything I want to if I try". We can't do everything. Some achievements are beyond our reach.
2. *Tells a lie.* "I am a beautiful person and everyone will love me". You may be a beautiful person, but not everyone will love you. A slight rewording of this affirmation and it becomes; "I am a beautiful person and I deserved to be loved".
3. *Expectations too high.* "I am going to be successful in this venture and make heaps of money". That may or may not be so. A slight rewording of this affirmation and it becomes; "I am

going to approach this venture with a positive attitude and will do my best to make lots of money".

If an affirmation breaks any of these three guidelines, then the inner child will learn to distrust the whole affirmation process. When creating affirmations, it may be difficult to know exactly what is the truth and what is a lie. It may be helpful to get some outside view of the truth by checking your affirmation with a trusted friend or two.

Some positive affirmations for singing are:–
1. "I have a reasonable (or good) voice and I am going to sing with pride and confidence."
2. "I will sing the best I can and I will be happy that I have tried my best."
3. "I really love to sing".
4. "I will use my singing voice to bring joy".

E. FUN THERAPY

Humour is important in therapy. Where humour is missing, therapy can be slow, too clinical, mundane and grinding.

With voice healing, humour is particularly important. Some traditional music and singing teachers that I have met have managed to take the fun out of singing. Most of us have stories to tell about the damage that an overly serious music teacher can do. In most cases, they don't mean to, but they become so performance oriented that they lose track that singing can have wider goals than just excellence in performance.

Excellence in performance doesn't have to be joyless and mundane.

The example of the two music teachers given in the first chapter illustrates that, particularly with young children, emphasis on excellence in performance not only can take the fun out of singing, but may also reduce a child's motivation to learn.

Fun therapy is designed to reverse this process. The basic principle of fun therapy is that enjoyment is a more important goal than quality of voice. Taking a fun approach doesn't necessarily mean singing loudly and out of tune, although this can be fun. It means that, in learning to heal and train the voice, an emphasis is put on enjoyment.

I know as a kid, when I was learning the piano, I hated practising scales. I guess it had to do with my short attention span. Scales were

"A little bit of fun is a powerful medicine" Aldridge (1996).

so boring. The way that I learned to develop dexterity in my fingers was to learn to play Scott Joplin rags – they were fun.

There was a secondary gain here as well in that performing the rags appealed to my show-off part. No one wanted to listen to me play scales, but I could command an audience with my rag time pieces.

F. TRADITIONAL MUSIC THERAPY

I think that music therapists should have something to do with helping ordinary people overcome blocks to singing and voice production. My experience with the traditions of Australian music therapists is that most of them are very narrow in the type of therapy that they offer. Some that I have clashed with are closed to new ideas. The music therapists that I am talking about seem to have put emphasis on developing academic respectability at the cost of looking for opportunities for helping a wide range of people in the community.

Maybe this is because the university training is in music departments where more emphasis is placed on knowledge of music rather than on knowledge of psychotherapy. My belief is that voice rehabilitation requires a much greater level of skill and knowledge of therapy than it does of music.

I am pleased to say that some music therapists, both here and abroad, are open to new ideas and, in particular, that music therapy can help most people, not just seriously impaired or injured patients. Don Campbell's book "The Mozart Effect" presents well the scope of creative music therapy.

G. THERAPEUTIC VOICEWORK

Therapeutic Voicework has been developed by Paul Newham (1998), and others. This technique encourages people to sing in order to release emotions and for personal empowerment. He argues that the singing voice offers a more direct connection with the unconscious than the spoken voice. Therapeutic Voicework is designed to "Animate self expression when a client suffers from immobility." This is an exciting area of voice development and is dynamic in its approach. Here are four examples of voicework techniques:

1. *"The free ballad"*. Have the client tell his life story in the form of autobiography. Then develop the story into a fairy tale. Finally sing the story as a ballad.

2. *"Free interval vocalization"*. This is where the client is not tied to the notes of any musical scale and is free to create their own free vocal improvisation. Because the client is not limited to the notes of a particular scale and can make any sound that they like. A similar sort of freedom is present in group toning.

3. *"From prosody and speech rhythm to music"*. A client who is able to show colour and variability in their spoken voice is encouraged to transfer the same colour and variability to their singing voice. This transfer is done in stages.

4. *"The healing song"*. A song is composed about an illness which includes making sounds which represent the ill organ or the situation that caused the illness. The composing and singing of the song helps in the resolution of the illness.

Voicework also addresses the physical aspects of body work and effective breathing. Voicework is relevant to both healing the voice and using the voice to heal. Newham does both. I will discuss further psychological healing aspects of Therapeutic Voicework further in part B.

H. GROUP WORK

Whatever the therapy style, working in groups can be a particularly effective way of developing your voice. As you learn to overcome inhibitions to making sounds and singing in a group setting, you will be faced with the real or imagined judgements of others. This makes a much more realistic setting to face performance fears.

The other side of group work is to experience the joy of singing with others. Singing on your own can be fun, but singing in a group can be ecstasy. One of the greatest pleasures that I gain from running my workshops is when I hear people begin to make harmonies joining with the voices of others.

I will talk more about the joys of group singing later on.

I. SYSTEMATIC DESENSITIZATION & VISUALISATION

One simple behavioural technique can be very effective in overcoming fear of singing. Systematic desensitization is the art of bringing a person closer to an object or situation that they fear without allowing them to get frightened.

In the case of a person who is afraid of frogs, the therapist would allow the client to move towards the frog to the point just before they begin to feel frightened. Then the client would stop. The therapist would use confidence building techniques so that each time the client could move a little closer to the frog without becoming frightened.

The principles of systematic desensitization as applied to overcoming a singing phobia are best illustrated by the case of Phobic Phoebe.

Case study:– Phobic Phoebe

Phoebe was a 12 year old girl when she first presented. She had a good quality voice and wanted to sing in the school choir, but was too shy. However, she was confident at horse riding and she often used to enter equestrian competitions and win.

The problem I faced in treating her was how to give her the same confidence in singing that she had for horse riding.

In Phoebe's case, I asked her to imagine that she was riding a horse. I helped her to capture that confident feeling in her mind and in her body. Then I asked her to imagine her school choir performing. She could approach the choir from behind and she would not be noticed.

At each stage of the approach, she was in charge of when she stopped, and she was to stop just before the point where she began to feel nervous. The stages of approach were:–
1. Observing at a distance.
2. Moving towards the choir.
3. Joining the back row, but not singing.
4. Singing very softly with the choir.
5. Singing confidently with the choir.

After each time that she stopped short of being frightened, I would do some confidence building with her. I had her imagine that she was horse riding and winning. I had her breathe deeply and steadily as well as stand confidently. After two sessions she was able to imagine herself joining in the singing of the choir.

Her mother reported that she was able to join the school choir shortly after this, and her confidence gradually built from this point.

J. NEUROLINGUISTIC PROGRAMMING (NLP).
THE SWISH TECHNIQUE.

NLP is a theoretical system involving fine observations of how the body works. One powerful NLP technique for overcoming phobias or specific fears is the "Swish technique". It is very similar to the technique which I have just described. If I were to use this technique in Phoebe's case, I would take her through the following stages:
1. Ask her to imagine the horse riding scene.
2. Get her to put a gold frame around this "horse" picture in her mind.
3. Store the picture in the back of her mind.
4. Imagine her singing in the choir.
5. Put a frame around that "choir" picture and view it like a screen.
6. Bring the horse picture back and have her make it very small.
7. Place it in the left hand corner of the choir picture.
8. Very quickly expand the horse picture to completely cover the choir picture.
9. Ask her to fully experience the confidence that goes with the horse picture.
10. Make the screen go blank and then put the choir picture back on the screen.
11. Repeat steps six to ten, five times making sure that the screen is wiped blank after each time.

As the horse picture takes over the choir picture, Phoebe should appear more confident and relaxed. Usually as the exercise is repeated, it becomes more and more difficult to imagine the choir picture. This is a sign that the exercise is working.

It is important when doing the swish, that the therapist observe the client very carefully and look for subtle changes. Sometimes it doesn't work well and modifications have to be made. The swish technique works particularly well with kids.

K. DANCE MOVEMENT AND VOICE

Dance and rhythmical movements can be very useful in the healing process. I discuss more about the role of movement in healing in chapters 6 and 10. When voice healing work is combined with dance therapy and other creative movements, there is a greater potential for the body to discover new solutions to voice problems. The reason for this is that there are more parts of the body involved and therefore it is more holistic.

The "Dance and Chant" technique is one that combines rhythmical dance movement with chanting (or toning). The movement and chanting may be accompanied by recorded music or by a simple percussive beat.

The chanting or toning should be integrated with the movement. Examples of this integration are:–

- When the body is upright, the pitch of the sound may be high and when the body is close to the ground, the pitch may be low.
- When the movement speeds up, the rhythm of the chant increases.
- When the movements are purposeful, the voice is strong and when the movements are vague or loose, the voice is weak.

The dance and voice combination gives the body a opportunity to integrate.

Dance, in itself can be a wordrerful way of relaxing, and relaxation will nearly always be good for the voice.

CHAPTER 5

Where to get help with your voice

It can be confusing to know where to get help. Here are some ideas about how and where to look

Therapy vs do it yourself

This book is aimed at giving an overview of remedial voice work as well as giving some self help advice. Voice work is one area where the effectiveness of self help is limited. The treatment of most voice problems will require at least some professional guidance and feedback. This professional help can be particularly useful if the voice problems result from psychological blocks.

When you "do it yourself", it can be difficult to know whether you are singing in tune or not among other things. A qualified voice therapist can give you feedback about:–

1. The various qualities of your voice, including singing in tune.
2. Any negative self talk subtly creeping in.
3. Body structure, breathing patterns etc.
4. Throat, neck and other tension.
5. Level of general anxiety.

A qualified voice therapist can also help overcome psychological and physical blocks to voice production.

Nevertheless, some self help can be beneficial. In chapter 7, I will describe various exercises that can help strengthen the voice and self confidence. In the context of self help, you can learn to become more aware of the following:–

1. Judging whether or you are singing in tune.
2. Listening for any negative self talk and changing it.
3. Your body structure, breathing patterns etc.
4. Your throat, neck and other tension.
5. Your sense of your own level of anxiety.

Also, you can practise self nurturing and you can provide yourself with a safe setting to practise your vocal exercises.

Psychotherapy vs a singing or voice teacher

Once you have made the decision that you need to seek out some professional help with your voice, it is often difficult to know who to get this help from. Should you go to a voice therapist or should you go to a singing teacher?

My advice is:–

- Choose a voice therapist if you know or suspect that there are psychological blocks to your vocal expression.
- Choose a singing teacher if you feel the issue is simply that of training your voice.
- Choose a speech and drama teacher if you wish to train your spoken voice.

A voice teacher would help you improve voice technique and give you feed back about the quality of your voice.

Speech therapists and speech pathologists have an important role to play in remedial vocal work. Many of these professionals also have the necessary skills to work with improving the singing voice. Some psychologists, psychotherapists and audiologists also specialize in working with the voice. Even some music therapists can help with developing the singing voice.

Short term or long term therapy

Once you have decided that you need the help of a therapist to work through psychological blocks in relation to your voice, you may wonder how long the therapy will take. Some simple phobias can be cured fairly easily in as little as two or three sessions. Issues arising from childhood trauma, nearly always take a long time to work through. These issues are complex and deeply embedded in the subconscious.

Long term therapy would be unusual just to just fix a problem with the voice. However, a person who presents with voice problems may have deeper issues of self esteem. The voice problem is just a symptom of deeper problems.

Long term therapy usually relates to building self esteem, setting better boundaries, improved assertions skills and learning how to love oneself. Improving the quality of one's voice is usually an byproduct of improving these other things.

An hour a week does make a difference

If you are in therapy for several months or even years, a relationship based on trust will need to develop between you and your therapist for the therapy to be effective. Some clients have asked me, "How can therapy do any good if I only see you for one hour of the week?" "The rest of the week I am on my own without your support."

Good therapy is not about the therapist being there for the client at all times. It is about the quality of the relationship when client and therapist are together. In a good therapeutic relationship, one hour a week does make a huge difference. Because, in that hour, the client should not be betrayed or let down by the therapist. The therapist is there for the client.

A good therapist, will provide a client with as close to unconditional acceptance as they can get in their adult life. In therapy, some clients experience this unconditional acceptance for the first time in their life. Where a client missed out on unconditional love in his childhood, unconditional regard, acceptance or love from a therapist can repair some of the damage caused by the childhood neglect.

Desirable qualities for a voice therapist

The task of finding a good voice therapist is not an easy one. Voice therapy is not a widely recognised professional discipline like psychology or music therapy. They are an endangered species. Fortunately, there are various voice therapist captive breeding programs in place.

In your search for a voice therapist, seek out the following qualities:–

- Qualified in psychotherapy, preferably a psychologist. (I admit my bias here).
- Caring, compassionate, supportive, and empathic (one who can get on your wave length).
- Good listening skills.
- Skilled in the sense of knowing their psychological and voice theory and how to apply it.
- Their ideas are not too way out, or too conservative for you.
- Good intentions and good boundaries. Intention is very important. If you are going to let a person tone you or take you through a guided meditation, then satisfy yourself that they are well intended towards you. If in doubt, be cautious. Discuss your concerns with the therapist.

If you put yourself in the hands of a person without these listed qualities, you take your chances. Some therapists can do more harm than good if they don't have the knowledge and breadth of experience to deal with what comes up.

Also, don't be shy to ask a psychotherapist about:–
• Their qualifications.
• Their experience.
• Their style and belief systems.

After all, you are the consumer and they are providing the service.

Remember, not all qualified people are effective healers and not all unqualified people are ineffective. Qualifications and experience are just good guides to competence.

The setting for therapy

When you find a therapist that you like, check out the setting where the therapist works. It should be relaxed and you should feel safe. It should allow for privacy and the chance to express yourself vocally without fear of being overheard.

Your new voice and speaking the truth

Now that you are on the journey to discovering the natural power in your singing and speaking voice, what are you going to do with this new found power? If you have always been a people pleaser who wanted to keep the peace at any price, then speaking your truth can be very empowering.

Enjoy your new found power and confidence. Begin to sing and speak confidently.

But! — A word of caution.

In the early 1970s there was that post 60s optimistic feeling about building new ways of communicating and relating. The Australian Institute of Human Relations was formed to help people relate to each other better. I became an enthusiastic member of this organization.

In 1973, Will Schutz, a psychologist and guru in the encounter movement, was brought out from California to run a week long residential workshop at the University of New England. Well over 100 people from all around Australia attended. The workshop was inspirational. The timing of the workshop was not long after the Watergate scandal and President Nixon's resignation in the USA. Will Schutz was preaching the message of "speaking the truth".

Like so many others, I was inspired. This was the answer to our social problems. I returned home to speak my truth. I spoke my truth at work. I told my boss what I thought of him. I spoke my truth to my friends. I told them what I didn't like. The results were pure disaster for me. I was in trouble all over the place.

I learned some valuable lessons from this:–
1. Know that the truth that I speak is my own truth and may not necessarily be right.
2. Examine my motives for speaking out the truth. Is my motivation to do good or am I motivated by power or the need to get even?
3. Think about the impact that my truth will have on others. Not everyone that I talk to will be aware that the "Age of Aquarius" is dawning.
4. Do not speak the truth with evangelical zeal when the outcome will do only harm and no good.

In my own value system, compassion comes higher on my list of virtues than does the truth. I lost sight of that for a while.

The journey to speak the truth is a valuable one, particularly for people who are not used to saying what they want. I encourage people to develop their power to speak their truth, but with the cautions that I have mentioned in mind.

Prevention of relapse

Once you have begun the journey of recovering the power of your voice, it is important to insure against relapse. To do this you will need to monitor the safety of the environment in which you sing or speak. If you have to put yourself at psychological risk, such as might be the case in public speaking, it will be necessary to do exercises to protect yourself from criticism.

One simple exercise is the perspex dome. When you are in a threatening situation, such as public speaking to a critical audience, imagine that you are covered by an invisible perspex dome which surrounds you. You can put your voice out through the dome, but criticisms and abuse cannot get in.

Join a singing group

One effective way of providing a safe and nurturing environment for your voice to flourish is to form or join a singing group of friends or a small choir. More about this later.

CHAPTER 6

Getting my Singing Body in Shape

The body is to the voice what the compressor is to a pipe organ.

The body as a memory storehouse

I have long believed in the need for a holistic approach to healing, even way back in the days before it was "politically correct". The more we learn about the subtleties and complexities of how the body works, the less appealing is the old idea of the separation of mind and body.

I can remember in the late 1960's, learning about research done in Russia on "memory in the muscles". The Russian idea at the time, was that information is stored throughout the body and, in particular, in the muscles. The brain isn't the only storehouse of what we know.

The stored memories of our lifetime are reflected in the way we stand, the way we breathe, the way we walk etc. How the body reflects these memories has implications for the way we approach correcting physical problems such as poor body structure, breathing patterns, tension in the neck and vocal chords.

Keleman's "Emotional Anatomy"

Stanley Keleman, in his book "Emotional Anatomy" (Keleman 1985) talks about how memories are stored in our body structure. He says that the "Human shape reveals its genetic and emotional history". The human body stores in its structure, significant "insults". These insults are traumas that may have been physical or psychological in nature. As a consequence of our experiences, our body developed a particular structure to reflect those experiences.

Keleman talks about four main body types; the rigid, the dense, the swollen and the collapsed structures. A body can have various combinations of these types, for example, a rigid outer and a dense inner. It is often possible to see at a glance what body type a person is. For instance, a collapsed type tends to be caved in at the chest, head pitched forward, hands held loosely, knees slightly bent etc. They have a defeated look about them.

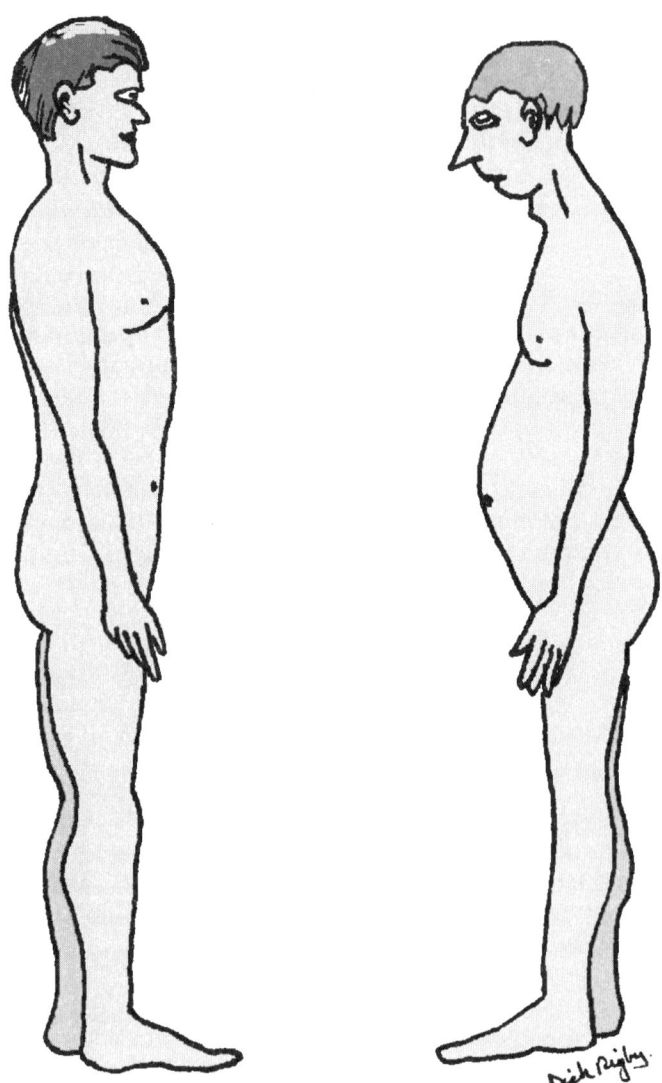

The rigid and the collapsed body structures

People with a rigid body structure can be said to have body armour. This body armour is in place as a protection against further insult. A person may present to therapy wanting to become more relaxed, but the body only knows one way to protect itself from an external threat. That is to remain rigid.

Keleman talks about how different organs compensate for insult. Muscles, for instance, that vary from the normal can be overbound (tense) or underbound (slack) in terms of their tone.

The extremes of muscle tone Keleman refers to as overbound or underbound can both cause problems with vocalization. The person with underbound muscles of the throat will find these muscles hard to control as the muscles will not respond appropriately. Overbound muscles will be too tense and not able to respond freely.

Keleman talks about how the body tubes such as the throat can be constrained and congested in some people. These people are likely to experience voice production problems.

Memory at the cellular level

In very recent years, there is growing acceptance that memory is not just in the nerves and muscles of the body, but learning goes right down to the cellular level. This concept is that learning applies not just to particular cells or organs, but to all cells. Deepak Chopra (1990 a) has brought to the popular attention this notion of memory at a cellular level.

Paul Pearsall (1998) talks about memory in the cells and structures of the heart. He tells the remarkable story relayed to him by a psychiatrist of an eight year old girl. This girl was the recipient of the heart of a ten year old murdered girl. The psychiatrist related the following account to Paul Pearsall:–

> *"Her mother brought her to me when she started screaming at night about her dreams of the man who had murdered her donor. She said her daughter knew who it was. After several sessions, I just could not deny the reality of what this child was telling me. Her mother and I finally decided to call the police and, using the descriptions from the little girl, they found the murderer. He was easily convicted with the evidence my patient provided. The time, the weapon, the place, the clothes he wore, what the little girl he killed had said to him ... everything the little heart transplant recipient reported was completely accurate." (Pearsall 1998 P 7)*

This is one of many stories in his book which challenge the conventional view of memory. The examples from Chopra, Pearsall and others illustrate how complex the storage of memories is and how relatively little we know about it.

Breathing and stance

Many problems with vocal expression in general, and singing in particular, arise from the way that we breathe and the way that we hold our body. These habits of breathing and stance are neuromuscular patterns of behaviour. Over the years we will have learned many dysfunctional body patterns and habits. The habits may or may not involve psychologically significant memories. Psychological significance gives the memories an emotional loading.

Some examples of dysfunctional habits that can cause problems with voice production are:–

1. Taking shallow breaths that use only a proportion of the lung's capacity.
2. Incorrect standing posture.
3. Incorrect use of the mouth and tongue. This can result in poor diction.
4. Incorrect use of the vocal chords. For instance making demands which are too much for the vocal chords. This is important particularly for a young person whose vocal chords have not matured.

In chapter 7, I will describe some exercises that can help to correct dysfunctional habits.

Emotional significance of habits

Dysfunctional habits may not carry a particular emotional loading. They may be habits that we have just fallen into, or they may be habits that were taught by a parent or significant other when we were too young or uninformed to know that it was the wrong way of doing things.

These habits are a lot easier to change than those that do carry an emotional loading. For example, the habit of shallow breathing may carry no emotional significance. A person can be taught how to take deeper breaths making more use of the diaphragm. This in turn will make a large difference to their voice production.

Those structures and patterns that carry emotional significance may require some psychotherapy of the type that I have talked about in earlier chapters. Or they may require remedial body work, which I discuss in the next section.

Breathing is the foundation to voice production. Most people who have the Keleman's collapsed body type, also have a collapsed breathing pattern. Their chest is caved in to protect themselves. Their breathing is shallow, they find it hard to get enough air into their lungs and their voice is often weak.

By contrast, the Keleman's rigid body type has a different set of problems. The rigid type has learned to throw his chest out and the breathing pattern may be restricted to the upper chest and consequently the diaphragm is not used properly.

Such profound body structures that Keleman describes carry deep emotional significance and are usually very resistant to change.

Remedial body work

Remedial body work is a therapeutic approach aimed at teaching or allowing the body to move in different ways from its stereotyped habits. This work requires the practitioner to have a greater level of skill in working with body structures and patterns than that required for just massage. Massage is just one of the techniques that a body worker will use. But not the only technique by far.

A conventional massage can help the body relax, but usually does not produce permanent changes in our body patterns. Body work is more holistic and is more likely to produce permanent change.

A skilled body worker knows about energy blocks and energy flow. She or he will know about how to make connections within the body. She will know about acupressure points. She will have an understanding of the subtle energy centres of the body and the wealth of knowledge from eastern medical traditions.

Body work may require the client to either move or remain still. The client is usually passive during hands on massage or manipulation, but doesn't have to be.

With other techniques the client may be required to move his body actively. Therapies such as voice dialogue, gestalt work and psychodrama require the client to move from one position to another. In this sense these techniques involve a form of body work.

Moving to different positions can be a very powerful technique. Voice dialogue involves the client moving to different positions to represent each of the different selves.

A similar technique is to get the client to move to represent his different approaches and attitudes to life or to different life situations. For example, the client may stand in one part of the room to represent himself as the part that is afraid to sing. He may then move to another part of the room to represent the part which is confident to sing. Much can be learned from the experience of moving from one position to another in this way. Usually the client will change stance and body structure with the move and will often not be aware of these changes.

Feldenkrais and Alexander techniques

Basic patterns related to breathing and singing will become very set by the time we are an adult. Even if you want to do it a different way, you find that you just can't. Feldenkrais and Alexander each developed techniques that teach the body to unlock and change stereotyped dysfunctional neuromuscular patterns.

Feldenkrais technique.
The late Moshe Feldenkrais developed a method by which the therapist can, in a sense, "trick the body" into learning new neuromuscular pathways. He has said that awareness cannot be taught verbally, it has to be experienced. He taught that effective learning is like that of the infant. It is self directed. The focus of the Feldenkrais technique is on the motor system. He viewed thinking and movement as part of the same system. He taught that to change behaviour one has to be released from the inhibition of an old pattern of movement before a new pattern of movement can be learned.

Some time ago, I heard the story of the dog with the broken leg. Long after the leg had healed, the dog still walked with a limp. The dog's owner took him out on a boat one day and about 50 meters out from shore, threw the dog overboard. The dog swam desperately for shore, and as he ran up on the beach, the limp was gone. The desperate swim had tricked the dog into changing the stereotyped trauma based neuromuscular patterns.

Alexander technique.
Frederick Alexander was an Australian actor who would experience recurrent voice loss during performances. He developed the Alexander technique which is similar to Feldenkrais technique in the sense of bypassing conscious control over changing long established neuromuscular habits.

He observed himself in a mirror to become aware of the fine movements in his body when he began to think about performing.

He noticed how his neck and shoulders would collapse as he started to feel anxious. He developed a series of techniques to uplift and expand the body. These exercises improved breathing and helped to create the senses of calm, harmony and balance.

Alexander taught the "Whispered aah" technique. The aah sound is whispered while standing in an upright and relaxed position with the neck free and the jaw slightly dropped. This technique is used as a way of freeing up the movement of the jaw and the neck and opening the airways to allows the stale air to be cleared from the bottom of the lungs.

Reichian Therapy and Bioenergetics.

Wilhelm Reich was a prominent psychiatrist/psychoanalyst in the 1920's. He developed a methodology based on body structure and was designed to help the body move more freely. He used the term body language for the first time. Body language means that the outward appearance of the body is a reflection of what is happening inside. He broke with Freud and psychoanalysis to incorporate the idea of the importance of the body into psychoanalysis, and the importance of physically touching the client.

He also used the terms "Body Armour" and "Character Amour" to describe the way the body protects itself. He invented the term "orgone" to describe a subtle biophysical energy which permeates all living things and is taken into the body through breathing.

Reich was the teacher of Lowen who went on to develop bioenergetics. Lowen taught that it was important to get your energy radiating out to the extremities of the body.

CHAPTER 7

Tuning & playing the Voice

Like any instrument, you have to tune the voice.
To most people in our society, singing in tune
doesn't come naturally.

The body is the instrument for the voice

The voice sound is produced by a musical instrument. That instrument is your body. Just like any other musical instrument it takes two things for your voice-body to make a good sound:–

1. It needs care and maintenance to keep your voice-body in good working condition.
2. It takes skill and practice to learn to play your voice-body well.

If we were taught poor playing habits when we were learning to play the voice-body instrument, those poor habits tend to stick. So as you begin to work through the psychological and physical blocks that have stopped you from reaching your voice potential, now comes the time to learn how to play the instrument properly.

Care of the instrument

People who abuse their body are also abusing their voice. Caring for your body is about avoiding any addictive behaviours such as excessive alcohol consumption, smoking, pushing yourself to the point of exhaustion. Caring for your body is about healthy life style, including healthy diet. Susan Sutherland (1995) says:–

> "It is important that you consider such things as food which may affect the sound you make. Citrus fruit, milky drinks, alcohol, chocolate, fatty meals, any thing that is difficult to digest or has an astringent or clogging affect on the natural mucus in the throat, will effect your voice."

This is good advice. I know several people who develop a lot of mucus after they eat dairy products. I am one of them. Excessive mucus can get in the way of voice production. But most things, except cigarettes, are ok in moderation. Some people with allergies cannot tolerate certain foods, even in small quantities. Pay attention to your own body's reaction to certain foods and work out what is right for you.

Let me state the obvious. Care of your voice-body involves a sensible life style, healthy diet, avoidance of addictive behaviours (particularly substance abuse) and the maintenance of an appropriate level of physical fitness.

Physical limitations

As mentioned in Chapter 2, there are many physical reasons that can prevent us from using our voices effectively. These reasons may be to do with organic damage or disease. Damage may be caused by scar tissue forming on the vocal chords due to an injury or due to a severe infection. Other physical problems with the vocal tract can be obstructive growths, muscle disease etc.

Be aware of any physical limitations that you might have and work within these limitations. Pushing the voice beyond its limits is not a good idea and can cause damage. Most limitations won't stop you singing altogether, but you have to be careful not to cause any further damage.

As we will see later, your sound can be part of your healing.

The feedback loop

A famous French doctor and authority on auditory neurophysiology, Dr Alfred Tomatis (1981) said that we can't sing what we can't hear. The feedback loop between the ear and the voice box is essential for us to sing in tune. In fact a feedback loop is not only important for the voice, but is essential to play any instrument. It is particularly important to play an instrument where the pitch is not preset, such as the violin or trombone. Feedback is not as important for playing instruments with preset pitch, such as the guitar or piano.

Sound is heard primarily by way of the ear. The inner ear detects sound by one or more of the hairs in the cochlea resonating in sympathy with the frequency of a particular sound wave. But sound can also be experienced directly from vibrations picked up through the body. This can happen when a particular body organ or structure resonates directly to sound waves entering the body through the skin.

More on how sound is received by the body in chapter 10.

When we hear a sound in our conscious mind, a wonderfully complex and rapid series of events has just taken place. These events are:–

1. The sound waves enter the ear and are converted to electrical pulses in the cochlea of the ear.
2. These pulses then pass down nerve fibres to the primary auditory receptive area of the brain where they are processed.
3. New nerve impulses are then sent to other higher processing parts of the brain.

The end result is that we perceive sound.

Sound is given meaning by the brain as it compares the incoming impulses with stored memories of sound. Finally the new sound is stored in memory. Your ability to retrieve this sound at a later date will depend on a number of factors including how and where the sound has been stored. The way the memory is stored will depend, in part, on how important the sound is perceived to be.

When we sing, we hear our own voice. This is the first half of the feedback loop. We hear our voice through the ear, by way of direct vibration of body organs and by sensing the vibrations from the vocal chords. As we hear our voice, we make judgements about the sound and whether we need to adjust it to make the sound more like what we want it to be. Most of these judgements are made in microseconds and continually. Most of them are made at a subconscious level. Much of singing training is about making us more consciously aware of these sound adjustments.

Once our mind has perceived the sound of our voice, the second half of the feedback loop involves the brain sending messages to the muscles that result in changes to the voice. We make many thousands of these fine adjustments every second that we are singing or speaking.

Most of us will have experienced what happens when the feedback loop is blocked by headphones. You would have heard the awful sound someone makes when they are singing along to loud music with the headphones on. The headphones prevent the brain hearing most of the feedback from the voice.

Much of learning how to sing properly is learning how to hear properly. This is the art of truly listening and hearing one's own voice.

Listening and habituation

If we attended to every bit of sound that came into our ears, it would blow our brain apart. The body has worked out sophisticated ways of filtering sound. The ticking of a clock disappears from our consciousness after a while and only reappears if there is a change in the pattern. This process of ignoring a sound is called habituation (or adaptation or accommodation). This process can be very sophisticated. For example, we may be half listening to someone who is telling us something that we don't want to hear and we don't take in what they say. But we still know when to say, "Yes dear".

We habituate to muzak (background music) when we go to the supermarket. But if it is a bouncy tune we become more aware and find ourselves singing along to it. Very quietly of course.

Auditory focus

We can generally overrule this habituation, by attending to something that we want to hear. But over the years, we have lost some of our ability to listen to certain things. We screen out certain sounds and never consciously hear them. Part of learning how to sing and tone is to learn the skill of auditory focus. To really listen and to really hear not just one's own voice, but other sounds as well.

The better we get at auditory focus, the better able we are to tune our voice. When we try to sing the same note (pitch) as that sounded on the piano, we make sophisticated comparisons. We compare the note from the piano with the note we are singing and make a very complex series of adjustments to our vocal apparatus until we perceive the two notes as the same.

Because it is such a complex process to compare sounds of very different timbre, it can take most people a lot of practice to become proficient at this.

Clearing the blocks

Chris James (internet 1998) talks about sounds like "OM" that will "Clean and remove our aural filters and reassure our inner ear that it is indeed safe, that we are truly starting to practise the art of listening". In doing this we may begin to hear sounds that we may not have attended to for many years. I believe that most people who believe that they are tone deaf are not really, but have lost the ability for auditory focus. When they relearn this art, they discover to their delight that they are not tone deaf at all. I have helped people who believed that they were tone deaf to discover that they can hear pitch quite accurately with a bit of informed practice.

Functional deafness

Functional (or elective) deafness is where a person is partially or totally deaf and there is nothing organic causing the deafness. Some refer to this type of psychosomatic condition as hysterical conversion. This is the condition that the girl Amy had in the film discussed earlier.

The functionally deaf person has a powerful subconscious part trying to look after him by causing the deafness. He may consciously want to hear, but the subconscious part is running the show.

People who wish to recover from functional deafness will need psychotherapy. Obviously therapy with a functionally deaf person is difficult, but many of the techniques described in this book would be helpful. In addition to this, the sort of toning that Chris James talks about would be helpful.

EXERCISES TO IMPROVE VOICE PRODUCTION

In this section there are a few exercises described to help improve voice production. A reminder from the introduction, that the term "partner" used here refers to the person who does voice exercises with you.

1. Exercises to improve listening

These two exercises will help you focus your listening attention.

Exercise:– Active listening to outside and inside sounds.

You can do this exercise on your own. It may be part of a meditation, or can be just sensitizing the ear to sound. Firstly, find a quiet place and sit in a comfortable position and listen to the sounds around you. Imagine that you are taking those sounds into your body and making them part of you. Really hear the sounds.

After five minutes, move your focus from outside to inside your body. If it is really quiet, you may be able to hear the sound of your blood passing through your blood vessels. Listen to your breathing. If you can't hear your breath, tighten the muscles at the top of your nose. This restricts the air flow through your nose and makes it easier to hear the breath.

Concentrate on hearing and taking in these sounds from inside and outside your body for between 8 to 30 minutes. Be aware that there is no true silence for us. There is always some sound going on.

People who suffer from some degree of tinnitus may not be able to hear certain sounds because of the masking effect of ringing in the ears, or background hiss. Low level tinnitus is quite common.

Exercise:– Active listening to a note.

It is best to start with some simple pure source note. A tuning fork is best, but plucking a guitar string is ok. If someone else tones the note for you, make sure that it is soft and as pure a note as possible. Concentrate on the note for about a minute. Really hear it and take it in.

Now before you get to create a note with your voice, there are some preliminaries to set up your body as a beautiful instrument for sound.

2. Relaxation exercises

It is important to become as relaxed as possible before you start the tuning of the voice. Use whatever exercises that you normally use to relax yourself. I haven't gone into the various relaxation techniques in any detail because they are so readily available. Most record stores will stock relaxation tapes and there are many good books teaching relaxation. Two books that you might find useful are Sutherland (1995) and Cheng (1991).

There are some relaxation exercises outlined below, that I have found to be particularly effective. To get the best results from these exercises below, make sure that you are wearing loose fitting comfortable clothes, and you are not likely to be disturbed.

Exercise:– Deep breathing

Stand in a comfortable position. Take a deep breath and let go. Do this again. Make sure it is a really deep breath and you are using as much of your lung capacity as possible. Repeat this several times. Be careful to do this slowly or you will give your blood too much oxygen and you may feel faint.

Exercise:– Groaning

This time take a deep breath and as you let go, groan with your mouth open. Repeat a couple of times and each time groan and imagine letting go of your body tension with the groan. Again, be careful to breath slowly.

Exercise:– Loosening up the body.

Twist and shake. Get into a comfortable standing position. Imagine that your body is a floppy doll. Shake each part of your body, particularly your arms and shoulders. Most of us hold tension in the neck and shoulders. Move slowly down and rotate your hips. Then shake each leg in turn. Be careful not to lift both legs up at the same time while you are standing or you will fall over. (Sorry!)

Exercise:– Massaging the kidneys.

Get into a comfortable standing position. Twist your torso from side to side and let your arms flop as you do. In this way your arms will naturally flop around and massage your kidneys with each turn. Your head moves with your torso.

3. An exercise to improve stance

Exercise:– The horse position.

Stand on some firm surface. Position your feet directly below you hips or slightly wider. Have your feet almost parallel but slightly pointed inwards. Bend you knees slightly out of the locked position. Tuck your bottom in and make your spine as straight as possible without becoming tense to do it. Move you hands out in front to form a circle with your fingers almost touching. This opens up the rib cage. Imagine your chest to be expanded.

Imagine that your head is suspended from the ceiling by a thin thread, keeping the alignment of your body. Imagine that your head is lifting up from your body and your neck is stretched upwards. This will open up your throat to breathe more freely.

This horse position frees the chest cavity to breath more easily. As much as you can, relax your body in this position and feel balanced in the sense that you are not going to topple over.

Some people also like to roll the tongue back and touch the top of the mouth cavity. This is supposed to help with energy connections and flow.

You can test the difference that stance can make to your sound. Sing or tone in the horse position and listen to how you sound. Then let your arms and chest collapse forward at the same time as pulling your neck in. Try singing or toning again and notice the difference.

Many people "pull their head in" when they talk as an unconscious habit. Try to monitor this habit in everyday life, and keep readjusting to straighten your neck and raise your head. Remember the Alexander technique.

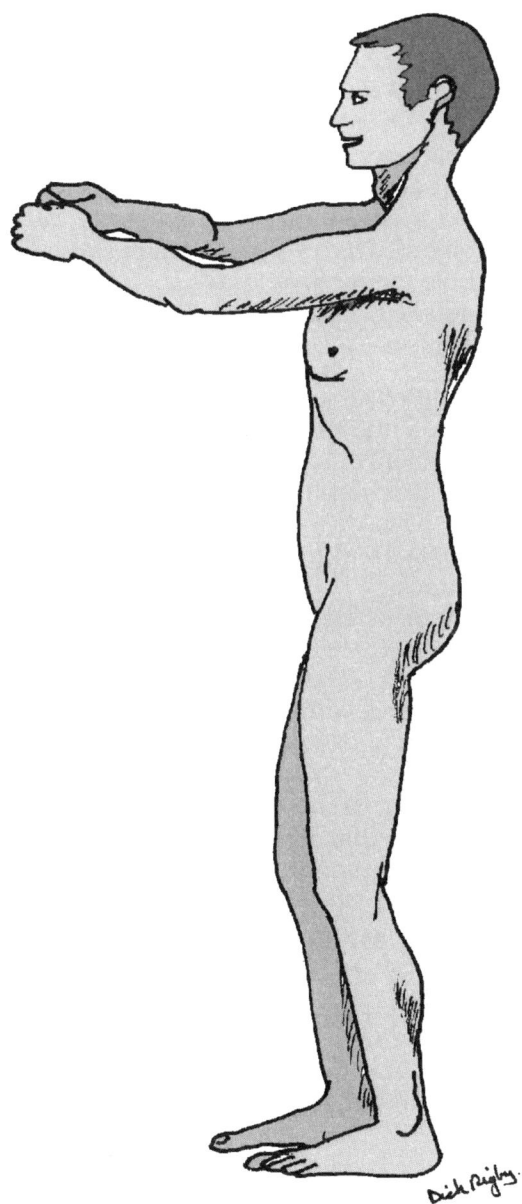

The horse position

4. An exercise to improve breathing.

Singing teachers have different ways of teaching breathing. Some recommend to breath high in the chest, lift the shoulders and expand the rib cage. Other teachers recommend to use the diaphragm to breath deep into the belly. It can be very confusing.

When I teach people about breathing, I look for where they are not using the full capacity of their breath. That may be in the chest area or may be in the abdomen. Wherever the weakness is, I help them to correct it. The whole body should be involved in breathing. Breathing should be relaxed, flexible, comfortable and give you a sense of being in control.

Exercise:– Using all parts to breathe.

Stand in the horse position and put one hand on your chest and the other hand on your abdomen.

1. Firstly keep the abdomen still and breathe by moving only the chest in and out. This will probably feel a bit strange or uncomfortable. People breathe this way when they are having a panic or anxiety attack.
2. Secondly, keep the chest still and breathe only by raising and lowering the diaphragm. As you lower the diaphragm, the tummy will move out.
3. Thirdly, breathe allowing both the chest and tummy to move. Allow a relaxed natural pattern to develop using both chest and tummy movement.

Make a note of what it feels like to breathe in these different ways. Develop a style of breathing that is comfortable for you, but make sure not to freeze any part of the torso.

5. Exercises to control air flow

You can control the amount of air that passes through your vocal chords by either varying the pressure used to expel the air, or by changing the aperture of the vocal chords. I won't go into the technical details of how the voice box works, but if you are interested, you can learn about these details from Paul Newham's book (Newham 1998).

Exercise:– Changing pressure.

Tone a note with a soft steady air flow. Start to increase the flow of air coming from your lungs. You may sense an increase of pressure in your throat. The sound of the tone may also become louder when you do this.

Exercise:– Changing aperture.

Tone a note with a soft steady air flow. Without changing the amount of air passing out of your lungs, relax your throat. The sound should soften. Then reverse it and try to constrain your throat. You should have the sense of having to apply more pressure to release the same flow of air as your throat aperture decreases.

The throat has to be able to relax in order to open up. One way of helping increase the aperture of the throat, is to imagine your throat as an open tube that is gradually relaxing and allowing for the free passage of air through it.

6. Exercises to improve voice control

Exercise:– The Siren.

There is a widely held myth that the voice has a breaking point between the upper and lower register. There need be no natural break point. If we experience a break point, it is because we have not learned yet how to guide the voice smoothly through this point. The famous Australian opera singer, Dame Joan Sutherland spoke of Maria Callas's voice as "seamless with no joins".

Chris James says that the breaks in our vocal range may indicate points of emotional blockage. We can choose to pay special attention to toning these difficult notes.

The siren (or glissando) is used as a loosening up exercise. The first part of the exercise is the "siren up". Take a deep breath and start on a low note near the bottom of your register. Then slowly raise the pitch of the note until it reaches the top of your register. This should last about the time it takes to let the breath out. Repeat this several times, remembering to relax between each attempt.

The second part of the exercise is the "siren down". Take a deep breath and start on your top note. Then slowly slide down. Don't strive too hard. Have fun doing it. It is just a loosening up exercise.

Some people have great difficulty with this. They may need some guidance in how to change pitch. One person that I was teaching this exercise to, just couldn't get the hang of it. She started on a low note, and as she tried to raise the pitch of her voice. Her body went up, but the note stayed the same. Something blocked her from changing the note. However, she was able to vary her speaking voice from high to low and back to high quite easily.

This would be a suitable case for the therapeutic voicework exercise that I described in chapter 4 where the client learns to transfer control and quality (prosody) of the spoken voice across to the singing voice.

7. Exercises about tuning the note

Exercise:– Matching the note.

For this exercise you need a partner. If it is not possible to work with a partner, you can record your note on a tape recorder and listen to it on the tape playback. This is nowhere near as effective as getting feedback from someone else.

Now that you have concentrated on hearing a source note, your body is relaxed and loose and you have learned to slide the note, the next stage is for you to imitate the pitch of a source note. It is a good idea that you get your partner to give you feedback about the note that you produce. Your partner should have a good ear for pitch, but he or she does not have to have perfect pitch.

As before, get your voice partner to start with some simple pure note and you listen carefully to the note. It is best that the note is within the comfortable register of your voice. However, the source voice may be in a different register. For example, if you and your voice partner are of different gender, the registers may be an octave apart. This adds an element of slight difficulty, but it can still work ok.

When you feel that you have heard the source note as well as possible, start to hum the note softly. Have your partner give you feedback on how close you were to the source note.

Keep adjusting to get your note closer.

Exercise:– Sliding up.

For this exercise also you need a voice partner. You will be tuning your note to match your partner's note. It is the same principal as tuning a guitar string. When I tune one guitar string to the note of another string, I drop the pitch of the "to be tuned" string down by loosening the tension. Then I bring the pitch up by tightening the tension until it matches the "source" string.

Ask your partner to pick a note. Listen to that note and then try and match it. Then slide your note down several notes, ie make the pitch of your note lower. Then slide back up to the source note.

You will usually find it easier to match the source note using the sliding technique.

Exercise:– A simple song.

Sing a simple song and have your partner listen to you. A common fault for many people learning how to sing is that as they go up to reach a high note the note will be flat (ie slightly lower pitch). If you concentrate your focus before you sing the high note, it will help to make it more accurate.

THE MIX OF SINGING AND TONING

The same principles apply to toning as apply to singing. If you are toning on your own try to be aware of keeping the pitch of your tone steady. After you have held the pitch steady for a while, then change the pitch and try and keep the new pitch steady. If you are toning with others, listen to the sounds around you and be aware of whether your note sounds good with the others or whether it sounds discordant.

It is ok to tone a note which sounds discordant in relation to other people's notes, but make it a conscious choice as to whether the sound you want is to be in harmony with others or you want it to be discordant.

Experiment – muck around – enjoy.

Volume control and voice projection

Some professional and amateur singers who perform on stage have one way of singing. This is to "project their voice to the back of the hall". Quite naturally, most of the "How to sing books" talk about how to project your voice. The books even teach you to project your voice when you wish to sing quietly.

But there is another way to tone and sing. That is to turn the sound inward. If you are using toning or singing as a form of meditation it is very helpful to be able to project the sound inwards.

One way of doing this is to make the sound "mong". As you make this mong sound, continue to sound the "ng" part. Have the ng sound in the back of your throat, almost inaudible. Take breaths as you go, but don't return to the mong – just the ng. Visualize the sound going back into your body.

Practise, practise, practise

As I said earlier, many people, myself included, have a thing about practice. For me, it reminds me of having to practise scales on the piano as a kid. But to learn to use the voice effectively, practise we must. The challenge is to find a way of practicing which is most suitable and enjoyable for you. Some people will prefer a morning routine, others will prefer to practise in company and some will avoid practice at all costs.

If you feel that you are likely to be easily discouraged, it may be useful to work with a singing teacher who can act as your coach, or join a singing or toning group.

SINGING AND VOICE TEACHERS

As I mentioned in chapter 5, it is sometimes difficult to know when you should go to a singing teacher (or speech and drama teacher in the case of spoken voice). Teachers can be very useful in helping with the development of techniques. But you will have to shop around to find one that suits what you want. There are vastly different styles that teachers use. As I said before, teachers have different ideas about the correct method of breathing. Some teachers will also spend excessive amounts of time on pronunciation and clear diction.

Some teachers are very rigid in their ideas. I like a teacher with flexible ideas; a teacher who will listen to how you want to sing. If you want to be a country singer, it may not be a good idea to be tutored in operatic style. If you want to be a rock singer, clear diction and pronunciation doesn't matter all that much.

I like a teacher who will observe how your body works when you breathe and sing. Such a teacher will work with you on how to improve your own individual style of singing, breathing and projection.

When I work with a person's breathing, I am interested to see which parts of their body they are not using effectively. I encourage them learn to use these neglected parts. I believe that good breath technique involves having the choice to use all parts of the body when breathing. It is being able to choose which parts of your body you need to use to best sing or speak the way you want to.

CHAPTER 8

The Performance

A performance can be a joy or a horror.
You can do something to make sure it's a joy.

If you want to, or you have to perform

This chapter is for you if you want to do something with your voice in front of other people. It is also for you if you have to do something with your voice in front of other people.

The task may be as big as performing at Covent Garden to a packed house, or may be as small as a family sing-along.

It may be as big as delivering a speech to thousands at an international industry conference or be as small as delivering a report at a staff meeting.

The most common problem with all these situations is stage fright, stage nerves or performance anxiety. I don't know of any performer who has not suffered from this at some time in their life.

Professionals have problems to

I know many people who have said, "if I only had a good voice my problems with confidence would be over". Well that "ain't necessarily so". Professional singers and speakers usually have learned the art of hiding their performance anxiety. Nevertheless, in the pit of their tummy, it is often there.

I treat both professional singers and professional speakers who experience performance anxieties. In some cases the anxiety can be experienced as tension in the throat and can result in voice production problems. A singer may not be able to reach the high notes because of throat tension. Or he may have a problem with chronic hoarseness of the throat.

The anxiety may be experienced in shallow breathing and the sense of not being able to get enough air into the lungs. This shortage of breath can result in you having to take more breath breaks than you should have to, when singing a song.

Dealing with emotions –
Connection vs detachment

One way of coping with performance anxiety is to detach or dissociate from the feelings. What I mean by the term detachment or dissociation is what occurs, for example, after a car accident. A person may receive a serious injury and dissociate from the pain. They may not feel any pain or emotional distress until later. It is a natural body coping mechanism.

Emotional detachment to combat performance anxiety has its advantages and disadvantages. The obvious advantage is that you don't feel as anxious at the time, and you can be as brave as you need to be.

The disadvantages are usually more subtle. When you dissociate from your feelings you create (or amplify) a split within yourself. This split has to be healed at some stage or you will not operate as a whole person. If you have dissociated from stage anxiety before a performance, you will need to connect up later and reassure the frightened parts inside that it turned out ok and that you did keep yourself out of danger.

Fear and anxiety will not be the only emotions that you will feel as a performer. You might be singing a very sad song, and you may feel moved to tears. But as a performer, you must be able to control the amount of emotion that you let come to the surface. You will need to make a judgement as to the amount of emotion that you allow into the performance of your song.

If you are too emotionally open you can become preoccupied with your own process and lose your connection with your audience. If you are not emotional enough, you will appear cold and clinical to your audience.

A good performer needs to maintain a connection with the audience in order to maintain a balance between his emotional expression and the needs and expectations of the audience. Even Joe Cocker, with his emotional rendition of, "You are so beautiful," would have maintained an awareness of his emotional boundaries.

A performer can lose the connection with his own emotions in other ways. For instance, if a performer is drunk or stoned on stage, he may be disconnected from his emotions. If he is drunk or stoned enough, he will almost certainly lose his connection with his audience. Many's the time that this has resulted in a performer making a fool of him or herself without even realizing it at the time.

Emotions and "Method Singing"

"Method singing" is like the "Method acting". The performer can show emotions, even feel the emotions, but not become lost in them. A good method singer is flexible and adaptable. He is able to be in a really happy space and then begin to sing a sad song and allow the feelings of sadness to take over.

The method singer isn't really faking it. He is allowing himself to feel the emotions that are appropriate to the song that he is singing, but at the same time maintain sufficient distance from these feelings not to be swamped.

Dealing with praise, applause and adulation

I have spoken about the necessity to stay connected with yourself in order to stay connected with your audience. When you are connected as a performer, there will be some magic occasions where you will feel "at one" with your audience. When this happens, it is a truly wonderful experience. You may feel that it is safe to be in a "heart opened space". I know of some performers who live for the buzz of being at one with their audience.

"Addiction to adulation" or "performance addiction"

"Performance addiction" or "Addiction to adulation" is the "love of the buzz" gone wrong. It becomes an addiction when the performer "hangs out" for his fix of audience adulation. It is like gambling addiction. The addict needs this fix. He lives for the high of being the centre of attention and he loses the ability to deal with whatever issues the addiction hides.

The performance addict will chase the praise and compliments to fill the gap left by feelings of low core self esteem and/or loneliness. But performance addiction leaves the performer in a vulnerable position, because if the audience stops appreciating the performer, he can feel abandoned and devastated.

Surface and core self esteem

The performance addict has low core self esteem. He may appear to have good self esteem and appear self confident. That is the surface self esteem. Surface self esteem is your measure of your worth based on what you do and how you appear. Core self esteem is your measure of your worth based on who you are. Core self esteem has its basis in unconditional love. The new born baby is loved for who he or she is. Just for being. If a child gets this unconditional love and nurturing, they should develop good core self esteem.

Surface self esteem is what you do – how you perform – how "good you look". If the audience is clapping, the performer will have good surface self esteem. The performer will appear confident, but this self esteem is fragile and always dependent on external judgements.

Yin supporting Yang

In terms of a Tao view of the world, I see that core self esteem is the yin part and the surface self esteem as the yang part. The yin supports the yang. Without a strong yin, the yang is unsupported and can topple.

Performance addiction and praise

Some performance addicts with low core self esteem are in a double bind. On the one hand, he will seek out the adulation. On the other hand, he doesn't really know what to do with it. He is likely to feel that he doesn't deserve the praise.

Some professional performers go through the motions of accepting the praise, and bow and smile, but when they do this they are totally disconnected with their own feelings and therefore don't connect with the praise. They are not really accepting praise or thanks for the performance, they are still performing. It is a difficult task to learn to accept genuine applause. Enthusiastic applause is praise coming from a whole lot of people all at once.

The best buzz of all is to be fully aware and connected with audience praise when it comes.

Case study:– Egocentric Eric

When I first met Eric, he was a full time professional singer in his early 20s. He was a very competent singer and had the potential to enjoy a rewarding career in the entertainment industry. He had low core self esteem. His surface self esteem was reasonably good and he could appear confident on stage and give a very professional performance. But after he got off stage, he beat himself up.

He derived his self esteem from his audiences. His support was outside himself and he didn't have the inner support system of core self esteem. This was very dangerous for him. He believed that his audiences loved him because he gave from the heart. What he didn't realize was the nature of his audience and what was going on for them.

His audience were buying a product or commodity that he was selling. Some of them just liked what he was doing. Some loved what he was doing and were emotionally moved by his performance. Some even formed a fan club. But those that loved him were devoted to the persona that he presented on stage, not to Eric as a whole person.

His audience liked or loved him as long as the product he was offering was to their liking. Once it was not, they would move on to some one else's product. Unlike his family and friends, his audience felt no loyalty to him as a person.

"You fooled them this time. They'll find out what you're really like. They are only pretending to like you."

Eric had become addicted to the adulation of his audiences. His surface self esteem was dependent on how much they liked him. He learned this pattern in his childhood. He would get attention for what he did (or performed) rather than who he was. He learned that his worth was as good as his last performance.

Eric's inner child was always hungry for praise because he missed out on unconditional love in his early childhood. He had no mechanism for giving himself the nurturing that comes with unconditional love.

He began therapy. His recovery from this "addiction to adulation" was slow. His recovery involved him learning how to nurture himself and to focus on how he was a lovable and worthwhile person both on stage and off. He was worthwhile just for being who he was. He began to come to terms with the fact that his audience were just purchasing a good product and they liked him for providing that good product.

Handling criticism

Handling praise is sometimes difficult, but handling criticism constructively is nearly always difficult.

Criticism can be:–

1. Well intended or malicious.
2. Well informed or ignorant.
3. Overt or covert.
4. Constructive or negative.

Of course, criticism can be any of the shades of grey in between. The art of managing criticism is to have the adult in charge. This is sometimes a tall order if the criticism is malicious, ignorant, covert and negative.

However, there is much to learn from criticism even if it is not well intended. We don't learn much if we only listen to praise and other positive feed back. Some famous performers have surrounded themselves with people who give only praise. The world of such performers becomes increasingly artificial and fragile.

If you feel that someone, whose opinion you value is being excessively critical, ask them to balance their criticism with praise. See whether they can get the balance 50:50. Ask them to make their criticisms constructive, not destructive.

Stay in your adult.

The need to show off

Some people need to show off. I have a bit of that in me. I was brought up that way. I guess that everyone who performs on stage has a bit of show-off in them, otherwise they wouldn't do it. A little bit of show-off or exhibitionism is a good thing, but one needs to know that there are risks attached. If you are like this, some people will be jealous of you and may look for an opportunity to bring you down. Again, the Australian tall poppy syndrome is about people not getting too big for their boots.

Before a performance

Self talk. Using the information in chapter 4, develop a dialogue with your frightened child and or your inner critic. With this dialogue, calm down the rising anxiety.

Positive affirmations. Use the exercises described under "Positive affirmations" in chapter 4. Repeat realistic affirmations before a performance, such as; "I am well practiced" and "I have done this in the past", and "I will do my best to enjoy this show".

Positive imagery. Imagine your success before you go on stage. Imagine your confident performance. Visualize enjoying the success. At the same time, a part of you will need to be aware that the performance may not go well, so that you are not naively surprised if something does go wrong.

Contingency planning. Contingency planning is being aware of what could go wrong and developing some plan of action to manage that situation. Contingency planning is not catastrophising. Catastrophising is excessively dwelling on worst options. Contingency planning should leave you calm and prepared, while catastrophising will leave you anxious and worried.

Relaxation. Using the exercises in chapter 5, make your breathing a focus for your relaxation.

Stance. Using the exercises in chapter 5, take your body into the optimal position for the performance.

Meditation. Use the exercises described under "The performer and meditation" in chapter 11. Attempt a brief meditation before the performance.

Prayer. For some people, a prayer works well for them before a performance. Trusting that a higher power will look after you can be very reassuring.

PART B

Using sound
to heal

CHAPTER 9

Using the Voice
to Heal

The power of music and sound to heal
is sadly undervalued in our society.
Things seem to be changing for the better.

Powerful force for healing

So far I have talked about how to develop control, tunefulness and confidence in your voice. These developing skills allow you to use your voice for pleasure and enjoyment. These skills also allow you to develop a sense of your personal power and being able to communicate this power to others.

In this chapter, we look at how the voice and sound can also be used as a force for healing. One of the strongest recommendations for using toning as a healing tool is that it doesn't seem to have adverse side effects, and it is usually an enjoyable experience.

Sounds to alter moods

We all know that sound can have a soothing effect. Nearly all of us have had early childhood experiences of sound and music as being soothing and reassuring. A mother sings a soft lullaby to a child. The mother's voice is a soothing tone for the child.

Music can evoke many moods. Music can be invigorating and can help lift us up when we are suffering from the blues. For as long as history records, music and sound have been used to help people to feel better and to alter mood states.

The power of music to influence moods has been used by music therapists around the world. They have used music to treat depression, anxiety states and many other conditions. Music therapy has became a specialist area where music is used to help in the healing of both physical and psychological problems.

Aldridge (1996) discusses the benefits of music therapy in treating a wide variety of conditions, and in particular chronic bowel disease, dementia in the elderly and people with chronic immune system problems.

I conducted a music therapy group in a psychiatric ward in a Queensland hospital for several years. I used the power of music to help bring patients out of their preoccupation with their problems and to help them connect with the real world. A mixture of music and humour in a group setting was an effective cocktail to get this result.

VARIOUS SOUND THERAPIES

Vibroacoustic therapy

In even more recent times, various forms of sound therapy, such as Voice Toning and Vibroacoustic Therapy have been used to help in the healing process. Vibroacoustic Therapy, as described by Tony Wigram (Wigram et al 1996) uses very low frequencies in the healing process. The low frequency sounds are transmitted directly into the body through speakers that are part of a specially designed couch which the client lies on. Special music is played at the same time as these low frequency tones.

Olav Skille was one of the pioneers of this method in the early 1980's and developed the "Sound Bath" for use with children suffering from a variety of disabilities. He reported improvements in relaxation and flexibility of muscle movements as a response to children given this treatment.

Alfred Tomatis

Doctor Alfred Tomatis (Tomatis 1981) reported that there are two kinds of sound, those that fatigue and those that energize. Gregorian chants are rich in high frequencies and are therefore beneficial in healing and charging the nervous system. Tomatis developed a method of using high frequency sounds to heal. Tomatis developed the "Electronic Ear" which is a special piece of apparatus which generates filtered high frequency sounds that can be tailored to the special needs of a patient. Tomatis maintains that the high frequency sounds generated by his electronic ear can be used to energize the brain by stimulating the cells of Corti in the ear.

Therapeutic Voicework

Therapeutic voicework was discussed in part A as a technique for healing the voice. Paul Newham uses various voicework techniques that involve psychotherapy as well. In 1993, he wrote the book "The singing cure". This title aptly describes his approach. Some examples of how therapeutic voicework can be used to explore and resolve psychological issues are:–

1. Complex rhyme and association. He uses rhyme and word associations to have a client create their own song. The word associations that are generated quite often reveal the subconscious agenda.

2. Singing the dream. With this technique, the client is required to translate his dream into song form. This process also taps into psychologically significant areas.

3. Voice amplification and active imagination. The client is encouraged to imagine themselves as some form of archetype, such as a wolf. The client acts this out dramatically using vocalization which may include song.

4. The voice movement journey. The client is encouraged to move and vocalize at the same time. He calls this the "voicedance". The vocalizations are free form primitive sounds. Psychological information, particularly emotional information, is conveyed in the form of non verbal sound. Newham calls the process "Psychophonics". The aim is "To experience the authenticity of the Self through the voice in a safe and non-judgmental container".

TONING AS A THERAPY

From the many forms of sound and music therapies that are used today, I have chosen to focus mostly on voice toning in this book. Voice toning can be effective using both high frequencies similar to those used in the Tomatis method and low frequencies similar to those used in the Vibroacoustic Therapy method.

Toning through the ages

Voice toning has been used as a healing tool for hundreds, even thousands of years in various cultures throughout the world. Jonathan Goldman (1996 P 126) says that; "In the ancient shamanic traditions of Mongolia, Africa, Arabia, and Mexico, in the Kabbalistic traditions of Judaism and Christianity, and in the sacred spiritual traditions of Tibet, vowel sounds and harmonics, ... have been used to heal and transform."

The didgeridoo is a very ancient instrument that has been used in healing ceremonies by Australian aboriginal groups. The didgeridoo is a tube like instrument that amplifies and modifies the sound made by the lips, mouth and voice. It generates many overtones in a manner very similar to overtone chanting.

Despite the long history of toning, and toning like sounds being used for healing in many different cultures, toning has only started to gain acceptance as a healing tool in modern western societies in recent years. The term voice 'toning' was first used by Laurel Keys in the 1960 s (Keys 1973).

Since that time, the term toning has been used in many different ways and there are many different definitions.

The definition that I use is:–

"Toning is the use of sustained notes to help with psychological and physical healing, with voice development, and to facilitate the integration of psychological processes. Toning can be directed inwards to one's own body, or it can be directed outwards."

A tone by any other name would sound as sweet.
Shakespeare (sort of).

Some toning therapists use a very wide definition include sighing, moaning and humming as forms of toning. Toning doesn't just have to be just for healing, but also can be for enjoyment or voice strengthening. Toning can involve one or more persons either passively receiving a tone or actively producing a tone.

The variables present in toning

The five variables which can be present with toning are pitch, volume, duration, timbre and rhythm. When more than one voice is involved, a sixth variable of harmony applies.

Pitch: The pitch of a note is the frequency of the vibration of the sound wave. The greater the frequency of the sound wave, the higher the pitch. A treble note has a high pitch and a base note has a low pitch. Pitch is usually maintained at a constant level for long periods of time when toning.

Volume: Volume can be varied from an almost inaudible ng sound at the back of the mouth area to a loud ah projected out.

Duration: Duration is the length of time that the note is sustained. You can maintain a constant note for a long time by continuing to renew your breath. Traditional didgeridoo players are able to use circular breathing so they don't interrupt the steady sound.

Rhythm: Rhythm may be used with toning on some occasions. The rhythm may be part of the toning in the form of a regular pulse of volume produced by the voice. Alternately, a rhythmical beat such as an accompanying drum beat may be used to support toning.

Timbre: Timbre, (also called the tone or colour) is the quality of a note. It is determined by the ratio of overtones (harmonics) and extraneous sounds. I believe that timbre is the most important of these variables in the healing process.

When toning with a particular note, the pattern of the overtones can be varied by changing the shape of the mouth and the position of the tongue. For example, an OO can be changed to an EE sound while maintaining the pitch of the note constant. The EE sound has a greater prominence of higher frequency harmonics than the OO sound.

Harmony: This concerns the relationship between two or more notes. The traditional barber shop quartet involves four voices singing notes that are in harmony. Voices can be in harmony or disharmony. If different notes sounded belong to one chord, the sound will be heard as harmonious. When notes are not part of the same chord, the sound may be perceived as jarring, disharmonious or discordant. But not all discords are unpleasant. Jazz and modern classical music can have discordant sounds which are appealing to many.

Definition of harmonics

Harmonics, upper partials or overtones mean the same thing. They are notes that are given off when a fundamental frequency is sounded. The frequencies of these harmonics bear a strict mathematical relationship to the fundamental frequency. The harmonics are usually heard as weaker than the fundamental note.

Harmonic toning

"Harmonic toning" or "Overtoning" is a particular form of toning produced by a single voice. The mouth and tongue are shaped to place emphasis on projecting particular higher frequency harmonics while sustaining a fixed base note frequency. Sometimes, the high overtones may be heard as a clear whistle above the drone of the fundamental frequency. When it is done well, it has a beautiful eerie quality about the sound.

These whistle sounding overtones can be heard in the "Hoomi" style of singing which is traditional in the Tuva region of Mongolia. The Tuvan singers have developed the ability to play a melody line using the 5th through to the 13th harmonics while sustaining the same base note. This technique is not particularly easy for most people to learn.

Undertoning

The monks in certain monasteries in Tibet, using a similar technique, have developed very beautiful and haunting sound called the "One voice chord". Jonathan Goldman talks about the ability of these monks to undertone. Undertoning is where harmonic voice tones of sub audible frequencies are generated. This technique appears to have much in common with the principles of Vibroacoustic Therapy.

Passive toning

Toning can be active in the sense that it is you who makes the sound. It can also be passive in the sense of you receiving a tone made by another person. With passive toning, one or more people can make the tone. The receiver's role is to just listen and absorb the tone.

The receiver may be asked to "just relax and enjoy", or there may be instructions given to help them form images. The recipient could be asked to move his body in a particular way while he receives the toning.

The passive reception of toning can lead to quite powerful experiences. It is important that, when using this technique, the receiver is made to feel in control of the process otherwise the experience may be disempowering. When I tone somebody, I let them know that the toning will stop as soon as they want it to. They can lift a hand as a signal to stop or pause the process.

The sound bath

The sound bath is a wonderful healing exercise for group work. A volunteer is asked to be the receiver and lie in the middle of the group and the group gathers around and tones this person. Those doing the toning can either place their hands on the receiver, or be at a distance using the palms of their hands to project their energy towards the recipient.

Again, I ask the receiver to raise their hand when they want it to stop or pause. This leaves the receiver in control of the process. I usually cover the receiver's body with a light "healing cloth" that has "wonderful healing properties" (or so I was told by an old monk from Nepal who sold it to me).

Sound bath

Just as with all forms of toning, somebody should have the responsibility of monitoring the receiver for signs of distress. If the person becomes distressed the toning should stop.

Most people report that the sound bath is a very enjoyable experience. Occasionally a person will report a profound healing experience while having a sound bath. It is always great to play a part in such a profound experience. On rare occasions, I have had some people feel uncomfortable and want it to stop, but I have not yet had anyone report becoming very distressed.

Of course, this sort of toning is not for all circumstances. There are some situations where I would not suggest giving a sound bath. An example of such, would be that of a person on certain drugs or medication. It is possible that for people with certain emotional disturbances, a sound bath could be distressing or bring on an emotional crisis. So far, I have not witnessed an adverse reaction yet in the many sound baths that I have been part of.

For most people it is a beautiful and enriching experience.

Also, the sound bath is a wonderful way of bringing a group together. It is not only the recipient who benefits from the toning. Most of those giving the toning will feel good about it and may even experience strong emotional connections and reactions. It is important to have sharing after a sound bath, particularly from the givers to the receiver.

Energy flow

I don't pretend to understand about how energy can flow from a person's hands into the body of another. My original scientific training taught me that "If you can't measure it, it doesn't exist". Despite this indoctrination, I now take the view that there is so much that I don't know about how the universe works. The more I learn, the more inclined I am to believe that this sort of energy flow does take place.

People have reported strong exchanges of energy during the sound bath experience. I wonder if this is the same sort of energy that is reported in the reiki experience. Reiki is a hands on healing technique that has become popular in recent years.

Active toning

Active toning refers to where the client uses his own voice to tone. Such toning can take place while the therapist remains silent, or alternatively the therapist may join in the toning. As with passive toning, it is advisable to process the experience with the client once the toning has finished. Active toning has the advantage that you can do it by yourself for yourself.

Participating group toning

Just as with the sound bath, other forms of toning in groups can have profound effects. The feeling of participating in a group that is toning can be quite wonderful and can be like the experience of singing in a choir when the choir is singing beautiful harmonies.

Many times I have experienced feeling emotionally lifted and moved at the beauty and power of being part of a group making a toning sound. It can be a very heart opening experience. I have found the effect most powerful and profound where people are toning harmonies and the sound is one of a complex chord.

More often than not, when a group toning for several minutes the sound will crescendo and decrescendo in unison even though there is no one directing this. It just happens.

I have found that there is something magical about being in a group that are singing harmonies. But there is something even more magical about being in a group toning harmonies.

There is something special about holding that sustained note.

Using toning with other therapies

Toning can be used in conjunction with many other types of therapy. Toning can be used in this way to energize, soothe, empower, integrate, ground, connect with others and more. Among the many therapies that toning can be used with are:–

Emotional Release Work. Toning can be used at the end of a yelling session to soothe and reconnect.

Internal Dialogue Work. During voice dialogue with a young part, the aware adult may use toning to soothe, comfort and connect with the young part.

Fun Therapy. Toning and chanting can always have a part to play in fun therapy.

Therapeutic Voicework. The making of vocal sounds is central to Paul Newham's work. I would imagine that toning is very compatible with his methodology.

Systematic Desensitization. Toning can be used as an anchor point and a soothing element with this work.

Dance, Movement and Voice. Obviously toning and chanting are very important in the integration of voice and movement.

Body Work. Toning can be used at the same time as a massage and can have a soothing or energizing effect, depending on the circumstances. Toning can also be used with physiotherapy, Reichian therapy and Bioenergetics.

Medical procedures. Toning can be used for comfort and support during medical or dental procedures. The effect can be to reduce stress and blood pressure levels. It can also help with keeping the patient grounded and feeling in control.

Aroma therapy. Aroma therapists will often use music in conjunction with the various fragrant oils. Toning may also be used.

Reiki. Toning may be used with Reiki under certain circumstances.

Toning may be used in conjunction with reflexology, hypnosis, colour therapy and spiritual healing. This list is by no means complete.

HEALING

A. PHYSICAL HEALING

Researchers around the world have reported quite profound physical benefits resulting from the use of various forms of sound therapy. An excellent review article by Crowe and Scovel (1996) describes the recent developments in the use of various sound therapies in healing practices.

1. Vibroacoustic Therapy.

The use of low frequencies in Vibroacoustic Therapy has reportedly resulted in helping conditions such as cystic fibrosis and bronco-spasms. It has also led to pain reduction in conditions such as lumbago, and improved circulation in cases of oedema.

2. Electronic Ear.

Tomatis reported that the use of high frequencies generated by the "Electronic Ear" have helped with a variety of physical conditions.

3. Primordial Sound Technique.

Deepak Chopra (1990 b) describes the Primordial Sound Technique. This is a method for returning the "distorted vibrations" in the body to a normal healthy state. He reported that an elderly woman who had been suffering from repeated attacks of angina, was relieved of symptoms the day she began practising the "Primordial Sound Technique". More about this later.

4. Cymatic therapy.

Dr Peter Manners (as reported by Goldman 1996) developed the cymatics instrument. This is an instrument that electronically generates specific notes which are harmonics of those "calibrated frequencies of the human body". These notes are projected into the body in order to set up resonant vibrations. Some of the conditions treated by this instrument include: anaemia, asthma, colitis, constipation, diabetes, eczema, glaucoma, heart disease, hernias, kidney disease, multiple sclerosis, sciatica, sleeping sickness, syphilis and tonsillitis.

5. Toning and overtoning.

Just as with other forms of sound therapy, toning and overtoning have been reported as having helped in the recovery from a variety of physical ailments.

Chris James (Internet 1998), reported how he was able to tone his friend's hand when a "window fell full weight across the back of her hand". As a result of sustained toning, there was reported pain reduction and less than expected swelling and bruising.

Campbell (1998) reported that he has witnessed toning reduce the effects of tinnitus, migraine headache, insomnia, and pre and post operative stress. He reports cases of toning used to eliminate acute pain following physical injury. He also reported other cases where humming can facilitate the healing of minor lesions in the throat.

Some of the clients that I have treated have reported quite powerful effects in response to toning, including the improved sense of physical wellbeing, reduced experience of back pain, an improved sense of balance, reduction in sensation of tinnitus (ringing in the ears), and improved quality of singing voice.

The condition of sleep apnea may be one that would respond well to toning. I would be interested to know if toning has been used successfully with this condition. Please contact me by email if you know of cases where toning has been used to treat this condition.

6. Combining toning with other therapies.

I think that there is an exciting future involving the use of toning in combination with other techniques such as Guided Imagery and many forms of music therapy. Another exciting area is using toning in combination with hands on body work.

B. PSYCHOLOGICAL HEALING

Reported benefits

Although I am interested and excited about how toning produces physical healing, I am even more excited about how it is useful for psychological healing.

There are many research reports about the psychological benefits of the various forms of sound therapy. Tony Wigram (1995) reported on Saluveer et al using Vibro Acoustic Therapy. Saluveer reported that "The treatment of clients with anxiety neurosis has resulted in improved self confidence, reduction of depressive symptoms, increased motivation and a reduction in acute psychosomatic symptoms".

Alfred Tomatis reported that high frequency sounds are particularly useful in the treatment of depression.

Clients of mine have reported psychological improvement and recovery in response to toning in the following ways:–

* Improved feeling of wellbeing.
* Reduction in the symptoms of compulsive and addictive behaviour.
* A reduced level of anxiety and stress levels.
* Improved ability to relax.
* A reduction in the symptoms of depression.
* Improved motivation.
* A better feeling of connectedness, balance and grounding.
* A feeling of being more empowered and more in control of one's life.

The treatment of major and minor problems

Traditionally music therapy has been involved in the treatment of persons with some form of debilitating condition such as mental retardation, dementia, autism, major depression and other forms of severe mental illness. Other forms of sound therapy have also been used in the treatment of these sorts of conditions.

Toning can also be effective in the treatment of these conditions. However, the traditions of toning in the western world have developed to deal more with the treatment of clients with less debilitating problems. Traditionally, toning has been used to help

with working through emotional blocks, pain relief and with the treatment of mild to moderate:–
- Anxiety states and phobias.
- Stress related symptoms
- Depression.
- Obsessive/compulsive conditions.
- Various forms of addictive behaviour.

Most of my therapeutic work with clients has been involved with these sorts of problems and conditions.

Serotonin tonin': Toning for depression

I have observed that toning has a great potential for dealing with depression. The latest breed of antidepressants are the selective serotonin reuptake inhibitors (SSRIs). In Australia, these go under the trade names of Zoloft, Prozac and Aropax. New brands of SSRIs are continually coming on the market. This family of drugs work to stop serotonin (a neurotransmitter), being reabsorbed as quickly in the nerve synapses. The net result is that there is more serotonin available for neurotransmission.

The principle is, the more serotonin, the less the depression.

I propose that toning, particularly of high frequency notes, may act to increase the level of serotonin in the brain. It is certainly a research topic worth pursuing.

Toning to heal the voice

One of the many conditions that toning can help with is the treatment of voice problems. These problems, be they physical or psychological can be helped. I have also used toning for the development of voice strength and control as well as the resolution of emotional blocks which interfere with vocal expression.

Toning for pleasure

Toning is not only useful in the treatment of problems and conditions, but is useful in helping to improve quality of life and feelings of well being. One commonly reported outcome of therapeutic toning is increased self confidence, particularly in relation to vocal expression.

Just as with music and singing, people use toning for enjoyment, recreation and spiritual development.

CHAPTER 10

How Toning Works

*There's a lot more to toning
than just going "oo".*

The resonating body

When we think of hearing sound, we think of the ear. The cochlea organ of the inner ear is a snail shaped canal lined with small hair like cilia. These cilia are of different lengths. As sound enters the inner ear, those cilia whose length matches the wave length of the sound will resonate in sympathy with the incoming sound. The cilia stimulate the cells of Corti which send messages via the auditory nerve to the primary auditory reception areas of the brain as described in chapter 7.

Sound can also be detected in the body outside the ear in the form of direct vibrations through the skin. We know that different parts or organs of the body will resonate to different frequencies in the same way that the cilia in the ear resonate in sympathy to sound. Back in 1974, Dr Hans Jenny's research (Jenny 1974) showed the effects that sound waves of certain frequencies and amplitude have on matter.

Hearing without the ear

Wigram (1995 P 21) pointed out that it is, "Widely accepted that most people who have severe hearing loss can feel different frequencies in different parts of their bodies. For example, very high frequencies are felt more significantly in the teeth and finger tips, whereas low frequencies are often felt in the stomach."

Oliver Sacks in his book "Seeing Voices", (Sacks 1989) describes how even "those with the profoundest deafness may hear noise of various sorts and may be sensitive to vibrations of all kinds". He describes how a woman could accurately identify a chord played on a piano by placing her hand on the piano. A profoundly deaf person can develop a sensitivity to vibration as an "accessory sense".

Campbell (1997) reported that "Helen Keller, the great educator, was both blind and deaf and learned to hear through her hands".

Randall McClellan (1991 P 38) describes the phenomenon that he calls "bio-physical resonance" as: "The body is a virtual symphony of interdependent vibrational systems of various frequencies and densities".

Toning allows time for resonance to develop

I believe that the healing power of toning lies, in part, in its capacity to set up direct resonance with body parts. With conventional music, the pitch of the notes are constantly changing. However, with toning, a note of constant pitch can be maintained for a long time and this allows for a particular organ or part of the body to resonate in sympathy for a sustained time. It is this length of time which allows for healing to take place.

This is the magic of toning.

Resonance at a healthy frequency

Goldman (1992) said that each organ of the body has a natural healthy frequency at which it resonates. Illness can occur when an organ is not resonating to a "healthy" frequency. He says that if one tones the right frequency for an ill body organ, it can lead to healing of the organ by returning it to a healthy frequency.

Deepak Chopra (1990) talks about how sound can be a healing force. His approach is based on the ancient Indian Ayurveda principles. These principles have been used for healing for thousands of years. Chopra makes the case that everything in the universe has a signature vibration. Each one of us have unique DNA with a unique signature vibration.

He believes that disease is caused by distortions in the healthy vibrations. As I mentioned earlier, Chopra talks about the Primordial Sound Technique as a method for returning the distorted vibrations to normal. A primordial sound can be spoken or chanted out aloud or just heard within the mind. The sound is based on vibrations that occur at a molecular level.

Ratios of harmonics

Nobody knows exactly how the human body interacts with toning, but it must be very complex. With overtoning, the sound is complex and rich in overtones. How these overtones interact with the body is a research question that I hope will be answered at some time in the future. It might be that a particular pattern of overtones leads to two body parts resonating at the same time, one to a low note and the other to a high overtone. This simultaneous resonance may lead to some healing connection being set up between these two organs.

"Hi Honey, I'm ringing from the heart."
"How are you feeling in the colon?"

What we do know is:–
1. Different organs will respond to different frequencies.
2. Overtoning can produce more than one powerful note at the same time.
The speculation is about how resonating organs might interact.

Individual differences

Everyone is different. A correct or healthy frequency for a body part for one person may be different from that for another person. People respond to different frequencies in different ways. In my working with toning, it never ceases to amaze me how much latitude there is in the frequency of the tone. If your intention is good, it doesn't seem to matter that you don't tone exactly the right note for the receiver.

Nevertheless, I believe that there are some situations where it is important to tone exactly the right frequency.

Possible physiological mechanisms

Just how sustained tones help with physical and psychological healing is not well understood. Some possible explanations for the physiological processes are:–

1. *Massaging of cell walls.* Wigram (Wigram et al 1996) proposes that the low frequencies used in Vibroacoustic Therapy massage the walls of the cells and thereby facilitate diffusion of waste products through cells wall.

2. *Release of endorphins.* Goldman (1996) has speculated that pain relief induced by sound therapy may be mediated by endorphins being released in the brain.

3. *Increase blood supply.* Maybe toning facilitates blood supply to a particular area, possibly by causing capillary dilation in response to the resonant vibrations.

4. *Antibodies.* Toning a diseased organ or body part may facilitate the production of antibodies.

5. *Immune system.* Toning may have a direct effect on stimulating the body's immune system in other ways.

The list of speculation could go on. We will learn more about how sound therapy works as more research is done.

Altered state of consciousness

It is well known that sound and music can lead to altered states of consciousness. Jeanne Achterberg (1985) describes how people in shamanic practice enter an altered state of consciousness via the medium of sound. Wigram (1996) reported that with the use of music with Guided Imagery, the client can move into an altered state of consciousness.

Trance in Bali

I have taken a particular interest in the traditional trance state which is part of many ceremonial occasions in Bali, Indonesia. Nearly all Balinese trance states are associated with music. This music is played by Gamelan orchestras. The instruments in these orchestras include metal gongs, drums and a variety of Xylophone like instruments based on a pentatoninc scale.

Gamelan orchestras play at ceremonial occasions such as at funerals and religious anniversaries. The music is monotonous and has a steady rhythm. It does not vary in volume or intensity. In this way, the music is similar to toning and chanting.

Studies at the State Institution of the Arts in Bali (STSI) (Suryani and Jensen 1995), have shown that the people listening to, or dancing to this music, can enter a state of trance. Those who enter such a state of trance in response to this music, report their experience to be deeply religious.

These studies also report that the religious context is integral to the induction of the trance state. The musicians who play the traditional instruments can also enter a state of trance. The studies report that there are "Associated feelings of peace, quiet, and happiness which continue later at home and last up to several days....".

Jane Belo (1960) conducted extensive research into Balinese trance prior to the second world war. She describes seven types of trances. Three are of particular interest:–

1. *"Occasional trances"*. An ordinary person would enter a trance state while attending a religious ceremony. Some among these people would seek out trance experiences. They would move from village to village seeking out ceremonies in order to be able to reenter the trance state. This may an example of addictive behaviour.

2. *"Fighting and stabbing trances"*. Young men would enter a trance state and begin by attacking a mock figure of a dragon with ceremonial knives. They would reach a state of frenzy and could enter a state of "compulsive seizure". When this happened, they would be carted off to the temple to be revived. Some of the men who remained would turn the knives onto themselves and start cutting themselves on their chests.

3. *"Child trance dancers"*. Pre-pubescent girls would be selected from a village for their ability to enter a trance like state. During the religious ceremony, they would perform "Intricate non

rehearsed dances in a sleep like state, sometimes balance on a man's shoulders" (Belo 1960). The famous hypnotherapist, Milton Erickson studied and filmed these dances.

Jane Belo makes the point that what would be considered psychotic or neurotic behaviour in the west is considered normal in the context of a Balinese trance. I guess the same could be said for the trance like behaviour present in some western charismatic religious ceremonies.

Suryani and Jensen also talks about possession. This is a state beyond trance where a person is said to be possesses by a spirit while in the trance state. In the Balinese culture, most of the spirits are benign and being possessed is usually seen as a favourable event. Suryani and Jensen say that "These trances and possession are expected, controlled and highly valued by the society because they help maintain the prosperity, security, peace and health of the community."

A person who is possessed may behave in a strange way, but this is not of concern, because it is the spirit that is acting through the person. Suryani and Jensen makes the same point as Belo, that such behaviour in the west would be seen as mentally disturbed and a cause for concern.

We in the west tend to be tolerant to a possessed person behaving in a peculiar way if we know the possessing spirit is Jack Daniels.

Brain measures

Research has shown that toning can produce a change in the pattern of brain waves from beta rhythm of 14 to 20 hertz to alpha rhythm of 8 to 13 hertz. The beta state is the mind's active thinking state in which we spend most of our awake hours. The alpha state is the daydreaming or meditative state. When the mind is in the alpha state it is clear and focussed and the body is relaxed.

Goldman also reported that music in certain forms can lead to this changed pattern of brainwaves which is experienced as an altered states of consciousness.

Crowe and Scovel (1996) report on a method developed in the Monroe Institute called the hemisync method. Slightly different frequencies are fed into each ear. This sets up a beat which synchronizes the brain waves from the right and left hemispheres. This technique is claimed to synchronize both hemispheres at the alpha frequency which is associated with relaxation.

Brain resonance and subconscious change

But how does toning affect the brain to produce an altered state of consciousness? Wigram (1996) describes how the human skull is like an acoustic chamber filled with fluid and sound is transmitted through the tissues of the brain in this acoustic chamber.

Goldman (1996) reports the work of Stockhausen who "was able to observe physiological changes in the skull of singers he had trained to create vocal harmonics." Goldman speculates about these resonances producing changes in the brain itself.

Campbell (1997) reports Tomatis as believing that high frequency sounds "generally resonate in the brain and affect cognitive functions, such as thinking, spatial perception, and memory".

Different areas of the brain or organs within the brain have different densities and structures. Because of these differences, parts of the brain will resonate in sympathy with different frequencies or different combinations of frequencies. The mechanism by which toning works may be by selectively resonating particular parts of the brain and not others.

Theory of "Neurovibrational Intervention"

It doesn't seem right that I could write a whole book with out inventing at least one technical term. So I have done it. My term is "Neurovibrational Intervention".

This term describes a theory that I am proposing for the effect that toning, or other sustained healing sounds, have on brain structures and function. Toning sets up direct resonance or neurovibration with a particular brain structure. This resonance facilitates transmissions along nerve fibres and across synapses within this brain structure. This facillitation assists in forming neural connections with subconscious systems that are normally unavailable through usual verbal psychotherapy.

In other words, neurovibrational intervention can access those traumatic memories that form the basis of our dysfunctional core belief systems. By facilitating changes in these neural pathways, the core belief systems can be changed.

Maybe the change occurs at the synapsc level where the resonant vibration alters the threshold for synaptic transmission. Maybe it happens in a manner that I mentioned in the previous chapter under the heading Serotonin tonin' by stimulating the production of neurotransmitters. Sustained vibration may even facilitate the growth of new dendritic connections.

The challenge for toning therapists is to learn how to develop the right type of tone to harness such connections to produce the desired change in the targeted unwanted behaviour.

Storage of traumatic memories

Research has shown that traumatic memories are laid down differently from other types of memories. There is a greater involvement of the limbic system of the brain. The limbic system is a central area of the brain that is important in memory storage and emotions. It seems that the different way that traumatic memories are stored is what contributes to making them difficult to access.

I believe that when a person is engaging in phobic or compulsive behaviour, they enter a dissociated state of mind. They are in a regressed or "childlike state" where assumptions and rules about life are governed by dysfunctional core beliefs. These core beliefs may be quite different from those held by the aware adult.

The neural pathways that operate these dysfunctional core beliefs were laid down at the time of the original trauma. The limbic system of the brain will be involved in the operation of these dysfunctional core beliefs.

The neurovibrational intervention theory proposes that toning of the right form directly interacts with those relevant parts of the brain.

Holistic toning

Of course, for effective healing to take place, other parts of the body that are connected to a traumatic memory may need to be treated with healing vibrations as well. In chapter 2, I talked about how traumatic memories can be "stored" not just in the brain and central nervous system, but also in the muscles. This idea of "memory in the muscles" is integral to the effective processing and resolution of traumatic memories.

Just as toning may facilitate contact with the areas of the brain that store traumatic memories and control compulsive behaviour, toning can also facilitate contact with other parts of the body involved in perpetuating the compulsive behaviour.

Toning resonance has the potential to reach all parts of the body where traumatic memories may stored. All parts of the body can be massaged by sound. Resonance can bring about changes in muscles, organs or even individual cells containing emotional memories.

Of one thing we can be certain, the healing process in response to toning is complex.

Healing phobic and compulsive behaviour

Most of my professional life as a clinical psychologist has been spent helping people recover from the lingering after effects of some earlier traumatic event or series of traumatic events. The after effects of trauma may take the form of a fear or phobia, or some other form of unwanted compulsive behaviour.

The phobia, set up as a consequence of a trauma, prevents a person from doing what they want to do. The phobia of singing is one such example. In this case, the phobia leads to the unwanted compulsive behaviour of "singing avoidance". The aware adult judges the situation to be safe to sing but the frightened child judges it to be unsafe.

In chapter 4, I discussed the link between phobias and compulsive behaviours.

In general, when treating phobias and compulsive behaviour, normal counselling techniques and cognitive behavioural therapies are usually of limited effectiveness. As a therapist, I can rationally explain to someone "until the cows come home" that their behaviour is not logical or rational. It will make little or no difference.

Rational argument does not seem to change this type of behaviour. Normal counselling does not seem to be able to make effective contact with the parts of the brain and the body where the traumatic memories are stored.

Toning and other techniques

Many techniques have been successfully used over the years for gaining access to the subconscious parts responsible for organizing these fear based compulsive behaviours. These techniques include conventional hypnosis, Ericksonian hypnosis (Haley 1993), Eye Movement Desensitization and Reprocessing (EMDR) (Shapiro 1995), body work and Voice Dialogue (Stone 1993). I suspect that toning works in a similar way to some of these techniques by bypassing the verbal processing of information.

Sometimes when a trauma is resolved by toning, the client is not consciously aware of how the resolution occurred. It is fine for a person to have desirable change without understanding. However, I have a personal preference for helping a client understand how the resolution worked. I believe that self awareness is empowering.

In the future, I would like to see more use made of toning in conjunction with other therapies in the treatment of trauma based behaviour.

Preverbal states

Toning does not require words to do its healing. This means that it is ideally suited for the treatment of any condition arising from a trauma that happened before the child learned to speak. A trauma suffered at a preverbal age would not have had words to describe the trauma at the time. The memory of the trauma may not have words. Early trauma such as birth trauma can be stored in the mind-body. Even prenatal traumas are probably stored this way.

Some of these memories can have a profound effect in adult life

A simple example of a preverbal trauma might be as follows:– A toddler was attracted by the sound of a whistling kettle and the child's curiosity resulted in him being badly burned. Subsequently he became upset at the sound of a whistling kettle, or even any high pitches noises.

The trauma is a simple conditioned response, with no words to go with it. The healing of the trauma may involve gradually associating a pleasant and safe sound with the sound of the whistling kettle.

Toning to access early childhood core beliefs

Toning has great potential in the healing and resolution of dysfunctional core beliefs established in early childhood. The trauma that set up the core belief may be preverbal or just as basic language is developing.

Case study:– Overweight Wendy

The case of Wendy illustrates how toning can be used in conjunction with other forms of therapy to change a dysfunctional core belief.

Wendy was an overweight woman in her mid thirties when she first sought treatment with me for weight loss. She was highly motivated to lose weight, but was unable to stop binge eating at night. It will be a familiar story to many of you. Wendy went to many weight loss programs and, sometimes she lost weight, but she always put it back on again. She was a weight addict.

When I used voice dialogue with her, it became clear that the inner child was in charge of the binge eating. The inner child was using this behaviour to maintain the weight in order to protect her.

As a very young child, Wendy developed the belief system that getting bigger as a way of protecting herself from being hurt by others. The core belief was; "Bigger is safer". This core belief manifested itself in Wendy's adult life in the form of body fat.

I worked with Wendy in the following stages:–

1. I used voice dialogue to help her separate the part in charge of keeping the weight on, from her aware adult so that these two parts could dialogue. She began to dialogue in a meaningful way to help the inner child understand that fat wasn't a good way of protecting herself.

2. I helped her to develop alternative ways of creating safety for the inner child as she began to lose weight. This mainly involved her comforting her inner child when she developed the compulsion to comfort eat.

In the course of her therapy, she was able to visualize hugging the inner child at times of stress and perceived danger. This is the time when she would normally have binge eaten. She used toning to comfort the inner child. She used a soft "Oo" tone and she kept this up until the craving to eat passed.

It is not clear to me what proportion of Wendy's dysfunctional core beliefs about size related to her verbal or her non verbal history. I felt that it was a mixture of both. I suspect that the gentle toning had a soothing effect on some preverbal part.

This may be an example of where toning worked on both the mind and the body at the same time. We will probably never know.

I do know that these techniques were effective and Wendy was able to lose weight and also to begin to improve her self esteem.

CHAPTER 11

Learning
How to Tone

---

*Here are some techniques
and exercises that will help you
master the art of toning.*

Intention and potential for harm

Just as I mentioned earlier, toning and other forms of sound therapy appear to be very safe. Any potential for harm seems to be very small. But if you tone a person, they may enter a state of vulnerability. In this sense there is a responsibility for the person doing the toning to behave in an ethical and appropriate way,

Intention is very important when you use toning to heal just as it is with most forms of therapy. Your intentions in giving toning should be to give healing energy.

Good intentions are essential to using toning effectively.

I have heard of one case where psychological harm was done where the person giving the toning had intentions to manipulate the client for a selfish outcome. In this case, the toning did not go well.

Toning, like hypnosis, can take people into a deeply relaxed and vulnerable state and practitioners should only undertake psychotherapeutic toning when they are trained to manage clients who enter such deeply relaxed or altered states.

The skills of toning so far

The exercises in chapter 7 would have given you some idea of how to breathe, hold your body in a comfortable stance, and open your voice to make as pure a sound as possible. You use all these skills when you are toning.

Fear of toning, or toners' block

I discussed earlier the different ways in which a person can be afraid of singing. The most common fear of singing is that of sounding awful and being embarrassed in front of others. This fear can also apply to toning. But the fear should be less when it is explained that toning is much easier than singing because you don't have to keep changing the note.

However, there is another fear that I did not mentioned before. I have called it "Toners' block". This is the fear of what psychological pain the toning might bring up. Because toning has the potential to reach deep into the subconscious, it has the potential to uncover stuff that we don't want to know.

Toning to heal is like any other form of psychotherapy, it will tap into the subconscious. If this fear is strong enough to stop you toning, then it is time to seek out a therapist who works with toning to help you work through these blocks and use toning to advantage your personal growth.

On some occasions, I have found myself going for long periods of time without doing my regular toning. When this happens, I know that I am avoiding something important.

One woman that I was treating held deeply religious beliefs. She enjoyed singing in her local church. She had a melodic voice and was often asked to sing solos. Music was very important in her life. She was reluctant to do toning with me because she knew that music and toning touched her at a very deep level and feared that the toning might undermine her religious beliefs.

She feared that toning might, in some way interfere with her relationship with God. I reassured her that the toning I do is designed to enhance her spiritual connections, and to support her relationship with her God.

How to change your toning sound

As you learn the art of toning a person, you will need to experiment with different sounds. The perception of tone is so subjective. What is pleasant to one person's ear can be unpleasant to another person's ear. You will need to be aware of all of the six toning variables mentioned earlier. Here are some suggestions for changing each of them.

1. *Pitch:* Experiment with pitch until it sounds right for you. If you are toning someone, check it out with them whether your note is too high or too low.

2. *Volume:* The loudness of the tone will depend on whether you want the tone to be soothing or whether you want it to be a "mover and a shaker". Sometimes a simple soft tone is enough when doing healing. At other times a loud or complex overtone is the right one.

3. *Duration:* A nice length for a toning might be between 5 and 20 minutes. It can be either longer or shorter depending on need.

4. *Rhythm:* The use of rhythm should be kept for "special occasions". Whatever that means.

5. *Timbre:* The quality of the note is important. It can be rounded or harsh. It can sound nasal or come from deep in the chest. Experiment to find the right tone for the right occasion.

6. *Harmony:* When more than one voice is involved, experiment with different notes. Listen to what sounds good and what sounds rough or jarring. When you become practised in finding harmonies, experiment with unusual chords and disharmonies

The worst that can happen is that it will sound awful. Don't be discouraged, keep experimenting.

There is no set formula for the right tone. Common sense is required when selecting a tone. Where appropriate, you should ask for feedback from the receiver that the tone you are using is right for him. Some givers are able to sense whether or not a tone is resonating with the receiver without needing to ask.

They are "tuned in" to the receiver.

Developing the skill of overtoning

As you start to get the hang of toning, begin to experiment with making overtones. There seems to be a lot of healing potential in using overtoning. For most people, overtoning is quite difficult to learn. There are not many westerners who can produce the strong clear whistling overtones made by the Tuvan singers.

To start with, find a quite place with good resonant acoustic properties. This way you can hear the overtones in your voice. The bathroom is often a good place for resonance. If not, try toning up against a wall so that you can hear the reflected sound. Start with the "ee" sound and then move to an "oo" sound and then to the "or" sound. The ee sound should be made with a broad tight smile, the oo sound with the lips round and protruding slightly. The "or" sound should be made by slightly dropping the jaw. It should be a smooth transition between these three sounds.

Note that as you change the shape of the mouth some high overtones can be heard. They will be weak at first until you develop the skills of amplifying them. You may have trouble hearing your own overtones.

You can change the pitch of the base note and get a different set of overtones.

Another way of creating overtones is to make a strong tone and curl the tongue back in the mouth to make the "Rhee" sound. Experiment with moving your tongue and lips while making this sound.

Be careful not to hurt your voice when making overtones. Some of the harsh tones give great overtones, but are too hard on the vocal chords. It is not necessary to have a harsh base note to get a powerful overtone.

Overtones of the non voice type

An excellent source of overtone sounds is the Australian didgeridoo. A well played didg' can provide a wealth of different overtone sounds and it can be used as a healing instrument. It can be a helpful and pleasant experience to tone in association with other sounds. It can enrich the toning process to have a background drone. There are many good CDs that can provide a background to toning.

Check your alternative music store.

Toning the chakras and energy movement

Chakras are energy centres located in, or on the human body. The traditional knowledge about chakras comes from India and some other eastern countries. There are many different interpretations. Some say there are five chakras and others say there are seven. Some say the chakras lie within the body, some say they extend outside.

There is a growing body of evidence to validate the existence of subtle energy centres in the body. I won't go into this, but for the purposes of this book, I will accept that the chakras do exist and they represent subtle energy centres.

Chakras respond to toning. There are many different systems for toning the chakras. The one that I have given below seems to be the one in most wide usage. Each chakra is toned in turn starting at the base chakra. As you tone the note that goes with a particular chakra, visualize the colour that goes with that chakra. Each chakra could be toned for about a minute.

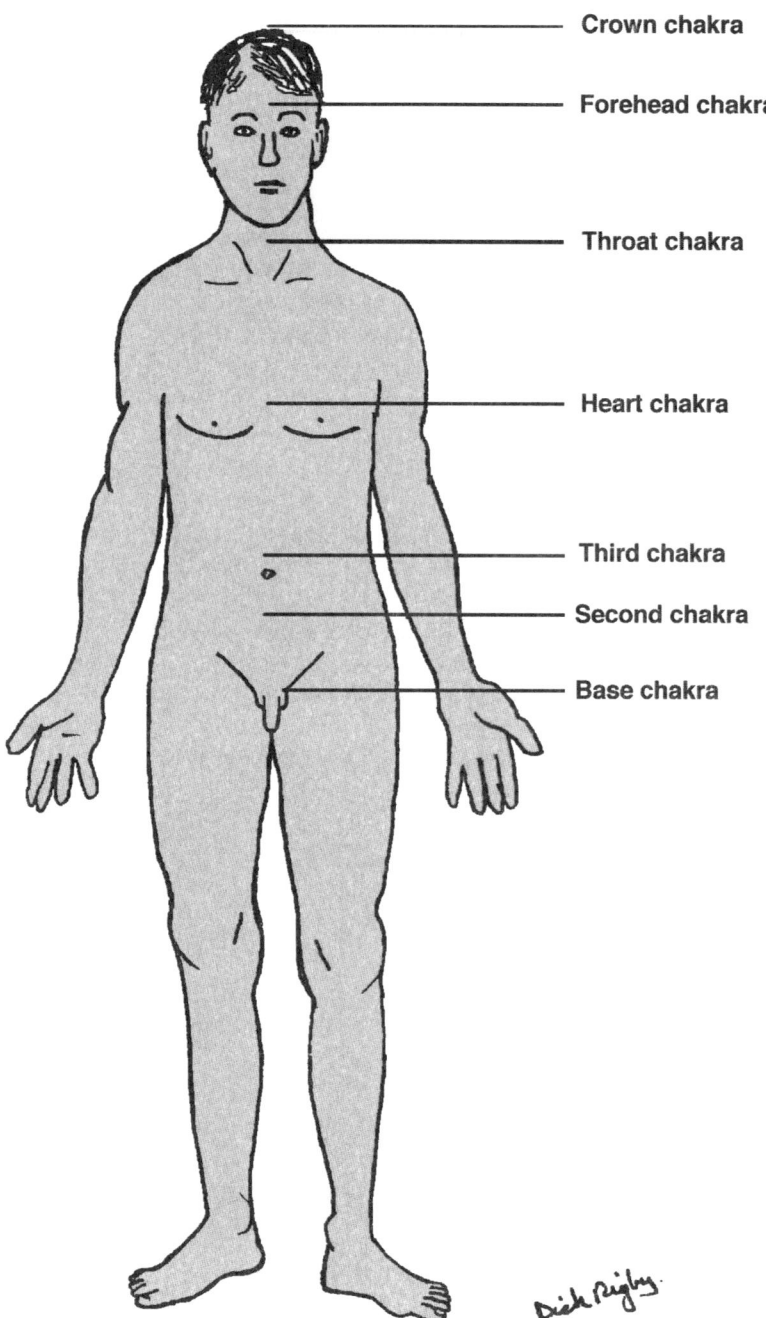

Crown chakra

Forehead chakra

Throat chakra

Heart chakra

Third chakra

Second chakra

Base chakra

First: Base (Root) Chakra.
- Toned with the sound of "oo", to the note of C.
- This is located at the base of the spine.
- It relates to the reproductive glands and it helps with grounding.
- Imagine this chakra bathed in the colour red.

Second: (Sacral) Chakra.
- Toned with the sound of "oo", to the note of D.
- This is located in the sacral area a few cm below the navel.
- It relates to the spleen and liver, and it helps with creativity.
- Imagine this chakra bathed in the colour orange.

Third: (Solar plexus) Chakra.
- Toned with the sound of "oh", to the note of E.
- This is located just above the navel.
- It relates to the adrenal glands and pancreas. It is said to relate to stored anger.
- Imagine this chakra bathed in the colour yellow.

Fourth: Heart Chakra.
- Toned with the sound of "ah", to the note of F.
- This is located at the centre of chest.
- It relates to heart, circulation and stomach. It is said to relate to love.
- Imagine this chakra bathed in the colour green.

Fifth: Throat Chakra.
- Toned with the sound of "eh", to the note of G.
- This is located at the throat.
- It relates to the thyroid gland and to voice quality.
- Imagine this chakra bathed in the colour blue.

Sixth: Forehead (Third eye) Chakra.
- Toned with the sound of "ee" with the shape of a round mouth, to the note of A.
- This is located at the centre of the forehead.
- It relates to mental functioning and to the emotions of fear and grief.
- Imagine this chakra bathed in the colour indigo.

Seventh: Crown Chakra.
- Toned with the sound of "ee" with the shape of a smiling mouth, to the note of B.

- This is located at the top of the head.
- It relates to the pineal gland and the issues of energy and worthiness.
- Imagine this chakra bathed in the colour violet or white.
- It is the point of connection between physical & spiritual levels.

It is interesting to note that several studies have found associations between notes and colours. The work of Skryabin, as reported by Aldridge (1996), found such associations. For example the note C is commonly associated with the colour red.

An exercise for toning the chakras

When I teach the toning of the chakras in a group setting, the instructions that I most often give are as follows:–

- "Lie in a comfortable position with your head towards the centre of the room."
- "You may choose to tone with me or just listen."
- "Stay aware of your breathing."

I then run through the instructions given above spending about a minute on each chakra. When the sequence is complete, I repeat the sequence of tones more quickly, this time spending about 10 seconds on each chakra.

- "Follow the sound into the silence."

There is about a ten minute period of silent meditation to finish.

Techniques for toning and guided imagery

The use of guided imagery in combination with toning can have wondrous effects. The type of imagery and toning used will depend on what the therapy needs to achieve. If it is designed to still the mind, it can be called a meditation. I will give you more information about meditations in chapter 13. The examples given below are of techniques that use toning and guided imagery in an active manner:–

Technique 1. To assist with the healing of a damaged organ.

This is a technique to use for self healing. An example of a suitable case would be a client with cancer of the colon.

Begin with having the client lie in a comfortable position. Encourage the client to begin to experiment with making different soft tones. The client can vary the pitch and the timbre of the tone until he feels that it connects well with his colon. Ask the client to imagine a pure healing light coming from the energy of the universe and entering his body. The healing light can change colour during the meditation. The light is powerful and capable of overcoming the cancer cells and stopping them from growing. Have the client maintain this toning meditation for at least 10 minutes if he can. The exercise can go for longer if needs be.

Variations on Technique 1.

A. The client can be toned rather than do the toning himself. The therapist would have to guide the imagery in between when she is actually making the tone.

B. The imagery can be more aggressive and the client could imagine tiny sharks or wolves in the blood stream devouring the cancer cells. The toning associated with this imagery would probably need to be more forceful.

C. A compact disc of meditative music, chanting or overtoning can be played in the background in addition to the toning.

Technique 2. Soothing the inner child.

Have the client make a tone that would be soothing to his inner child. Experiment with high and low register sounds. The client imagines nurturing his inner child, holding the child in his arms. He strokes the hair of the child and takes the child to a safe and protected place. This may be a magic garden full of beautiful light and colour where the child can play safely. This meditation could last from 10 to 20 minutes and the client should pick his own time to finish.

An example of this type of meditation is given in more detail at the end of chapter 13.

Technique 3. Trauma recovery for the inner child.

This meditation can be used for the adult to rescue the child from a traumatic situation.

As an example, the trauma that the client remembers was being bullied as a child. The guided imagery would be to have the client enter into his "aware adult" state. It is very important that the client gets into a strong adult place first. He may need some guidance to achieve this just as was the case with Phoebe and the horse riding picture in chapter 4.

The client would then go back in time and rescue the child by telling the bullying children to go away and taking the child to some safe place. I find that with this type of imagery, it is better to rehearse the scenario beforehand. Once an overall strategy is agreed on, the client begins the imagery journey. While the client is doing the rescuing of the child in his imagination, the therapist may provide a soothing tone or background music.

·

Singing and Toning for Life

CHAPTER 12

Sex

Singing and sex.
Now there's a good idea.

Holistic sex and singing

I added this chapter about sex in the hope of selling more books.

Well not really. How could I talk about holistic singing without talking about sex and romance? Sex, love, music and singing have been bedfellows since the beginning of time. In this chapter, we will look at sex in the romantic sense, in the physical sense, and in the gender sense.

Romancing the tone. Vocalization & courtship

Vocalization is part of courtship for a wide variety of animals, from song birds to whales. When we sing a romantic song, we are just another animal doing our courtship thing. But, because we have a sophisticated language and a wide vocal range, we are able to use our courtship singing, poetry and music in a complex and varied way. Despite the wide cultural differences in vocal courtship patterns, singing as a form of courtship seems to be present in most, if not all cultures.

But we humans are very clever. We can not only sing and woo our beloved, but we can use musical instruments. The variety and complexity of the romantic message is increased again.

Nobody knows what the first musical instrument was, but it was probably some sort of percussion instrument. It may have been a drum. Drums are used in many tribal societies in fertility and courtship rituals.

The beating of the drum can have the effects of inducing a trance and increasing the level of sexual excitation. It may be that frenzied fertility dances have a evolutionary significance in terms of bringing on ovulation and thereby increasing the possibility of conception.

Campbell (1997) reports that the world's oldest known musical instrument is a bone flute from between 43,000 and 82,000 years old.

Since the beginning of written history, musical instruments have become more and more sophisticated. For me, the pinnacle for the romantic love song was reached centuries ago when the bard sang a love song accompanied on the lute.

But if your taste is to get romantically turned on by heavy metal rock, good luck to you.

Electronic instruments

Big changes have happened to music this century. Humans have learned to play the most versatile and variable instruments of all time; electronic instruments. Electronic instruments fall into two categories:– Those that enhance our own musical creations, and those that allow us to play other people's creations.

1. Enhancement of our own creation

A. Voice enhancement.

The microphone and amplifier electronically enhance the voice. This has meant that one person can give his romantic message to a wider audience at one time. I guess that this could have an evolutionary significance. The performer can enhance his voice even further by various electronic gimmicks such as echo effects.

We live in an age where the quality of a voice can be considerably improved with the help of some electronic gadgetry. I state the obvious when I say that electronic tinkering is not really a substitute for learning to sing properly.

B. Instrument enhancement.

The instrumentalist of today who wishes to accompany his love song is no longer limited to the drums and lute. He can now be part of a band playing to his loved one while she is in the middle of a 30,000 person audience with stacks of megawatt speakers blasting out ear destroying sound. The effect is the same if the loved one is romantically captured by the music.

2. Canned romance

This century we have been liberated from the drag of having to perform our own love songs or hiring a bard to do the job. We can achieve an almost as good effect by putting on our favourite CD for that romantic candle-lit dinner. Playing someone else's song and music has the advantage of freeing us to concentrate our full focus on the serious business of courtship.

The disadvantage is that romantic music is relegated to the background. The challenge to create our own original musical endeavors has been replaced by recorded music. I am concerned that the free and cheap availability of high quality electronic music may be taking away the incentive for young people to learn to make their own music. That is, to learn to sing, write romantic poetry and songs, as well as to learn to play an instrument.

Poetry, love songs and romance

There is something about a love song that goes straight to the heart when the music and the lyrics blend together beautifully. But some music or lyrics can stand alone. Mantovani wrote romantic music that is beautiful even without lyrics. The poetry of Wordsworth can stand alone without music. For my taste, the combination of music and lyrics is the most romantically powerful.

A romantic song, music or poetry has the capacity to activate passion. Passion is the driving energy for romance. Most popular songs have to do with love and romance. I guess that music and singing will always have an important part to play in that business that leads up to sexual procreation.

However, if a person has a pleasant singing voice but is too afraid to use this voice, then a whole powerful area of romantic communication is closed off to them. Such was the case for Ruth.

Case study:– Reticent Ruth.

Ruth was 23 years old when she met Ron. She had a soft and very melodic voice. As a teenager, she learned the guitar and would sing to herself in her room. Romantic songs of course.

Ruth did not tell Ron that she sang until they had been seeing each other for two years. She then went to a voice development workshop. As a result of this, her confidence in her singing voice improved. She came home from the workshop and gathered the courage to ask Ron if he wanted to hear her sing to him. He was both surprised and pleased and said that he did. She sung him one of her deep and meaningful songs from her teenage years. He was blown away.

This was the beginning of a whole new dimension to their romantic relationship. Her confidence increased with encouragement from Ron and she went on to write songs of her own.

Toning for sexual dysfunction

We know that some music can be erotic and can result in physical arousal. There does not seem to be much literature about in the music therapy area about how music can be put to good effect to help resolve sexual dysfunction. This is surely an important area. Sexual problems can range from those that are mainly physical to those that are mainly psychological. An example of a primarily physical problem is the impaired erectile functioning of the penis due to faulty functioning of the valves.

Examples of problems that are mainly psychological in nature are premature ejaculation in males, or vaginismus (involuntary contraction of the vaginal muscles) in females.

Could you imagine a music therapist playing "the Stripper" while flashing X-rated overhead slides? Anything is possible.

Toning for arousal.

The area that particularly interests me is how toning and music can be used to assist with recovery from sexual dysfunction. The sexual dysfunction may be either primarily physical or psychological in nature. Most of the clients that have come to me seeking help with some sexual dysfunction have an underlying psychological cause rather than a physical one.

I believe that toning has wonderful potential in the healing of sexual dysfunction. If a sexual organ or system is not functioning, toning this organ or system may assist its return to healthy functioning. At a physical level, the toning may facilitate the blood supply to an organ, or any of the other possible physiological effects discussed earlier.

Blocked eustachian tubes and endometriosis are two examples of conditions that are clearly physical in nature, but may have underlying psychological contributions. Blocked eustachian tubes is a serious condition that can lead to infertility. Endometriosis is the presence of uterine lining forming adhesions to other organs, or the formation of cysts. It can be a very painful and distressing condition.

Toning can be used to help in recovery from these conditions.

The tone should be directed towards the abdominal area. The giver does not have to be particularly physically close to the recipient, and should be no closer than is comfortable for the recipient. It is important that the recipient feel totally safe and comfortable with the process, and doesn't feel that the toning is intrusive, otherwise the exercise will be counterproductive.

The toning may facilitate the breaking up of excessive connective tissue in the same way that ultrasound is used to break up kidney stones.

Toning is not a magic cure for problems of sexual dysfunction or infertility, but I believe that it is a useful adjunct to other therapies. Toning by someone having an appropriate level of expertise, and with good intentions, will almost certainly do no harm.

Where problems have been caused by sexually related psychological trauma, toning can be useful in recovery. Sexually related psychological trauma can result from sexual abuse or sexual assault.

There is nothing particularly new in the healing qualities of toning if you compare it to the soothing effect of a lullaby or love song.

Voices from Mars and voices from Venus: Singing as a gender issue

Voices from Mars and voices from Venus is, of course a take from John Gray's book "Men are from Mars and Women are from Venus". In the Australian culture, the voice experience is usually quite different for men and for women. This differentiation starts when we are very young.

Children are taught gender roles at a very early age. The influences that cause this differentiation are often quite subtle. The following is a comparison between Mars and Venus values in the developing voices of the average Australian child:–

MASCULINE VOICE TRAITS	FEMININE VOICE TRAITS
Loud	Soft
Aggressive	Passive
Harsh	Melodic
Don't sing	It is ok to sing
Speak out	Don't speak out

In workshops on singing and voice development that I run, I consistently get twice to four times as many women attending as men. By the time Australian men and women reach adulthood, the singing gender patterns are well and truly established.

Boys often learn that singing is "sissy" and belonging to the school choir is worth less than belonging to the school football team. It is ok for girls to sing and belong to the school choir, but they are discouraged from speaking out forcefully.

Men's issues

This "sissy" label that most boys attach to singing means that singing has been attributed feminine qualities. Nearly all boys don't want to do something that makes them appear to be feminine. Sadly in Australia, the cultural cringe that men have when it comes to singing starts at a very young age. I believe that the men's movement should make more of the right to sing without fear as a men's issue.

What is true for Australia is not necessarily true for other cultures. The traditions for male singing are different in countries such as Ireland and Wales. In these countries, men singing is an honoured tradition. In Wales you can be a tough coal miner and hold your head high if you belong to the local choir.

Boys face a further difficulty when their voices break. This coincides with a period when boys are very self conscious and the thought of one's voice cracking in the middle of a song can be embarrassing.

It is interesting that most rock band singers seem to be men. I guess that singing in a rock band is a macho thing to do.

Women's issues

Many women that I treat have problems with throat tension. Most of them have been told, from an early age, to "Hold your tongue" and "Pull your head in". The women's movement has had a great influence on reversing the effect of these negative messages. Speaking out and being heard has certainly become a woman's issue over the last thirty years.

Singing and remedial voice work can be a way to help overcome throat tension that is the consequence of the introjection of these negative messages. A woman who loves singing can learn how to sing loudly and with confidence.

This can flow over to help them learn to speak confidently out as well.

Changing stereotypes

These gender stereotypes appear to be slowly changing toward more gender equality in relation to voice issues. There seems to be a movement towards the idea that each person has the right to find the form of vocal expression that is right for them.

CHAPTER 13

Meditation & Lifestyle

*Meditation and toning go together really well.
I can't understand why most meditations
are done silently.*

Benefits of meditation

Meditation is a beautiful thing. There is no shortage of modern research to show the benefits of meditation to both physical and psychological healing and well being. The well known benefits are muscle relaxation and greater peace of mind. But meditation has also been shown to have a wide range of health benefits including:–

• Improved blood circulation.
• Reducing blood pressure.
• Improved immune system.
• Improvements to the digestive system.
• Balancing of energy throughout the body.

There are of course many other health benefits that derive from meditation. Many people, myself included, believe that meditation can assist in curing diseases such as asthma, chronic fatigue syndrome and cancer.

The chanting monks

The energizing effects of toning, chanting and meditation can be quite profound. The story of Dr Alfred Tomatis and the chanting Benedictine monks has been told many times, but it's good enough to be told again.

The monks of a Benedictine monastery in France had a tradition of meeting eight to nine times a day to chant Gregorian chants for between ten and twenty minutes. These monks thrived on as little as three to four hours sleep a night and had few health problems. After the Second Vatican Council, the Abbot in charge of the monastery decided to stop the chanting in a move to modernize the monastery.

Soon after the chanting stopped, the monks started to suffer from fatigue and depression and they were sleeping for long hours. Various doctors and experts were brought in to fix the problem. They changed diet, routines and anything else they could think of. But all to no avail. Dr Tomatis was brought in and he recommended restoring the monastery to the previous pattern of chanting.

It took only several months for the monks to return to their health, well being and vitality. Maybe the monks' demise was caused by the stopping of the chanting. An additional cause could have been the radical disruption to the monks routine. Who knows. But it's a good story in favour of the benefits of chanting.

Dr Tomatis used this story to illustrate the energizing effects of high frequency vibrations presents in the chants.

"Take three Gregorian Chants twice daily before meals".

The meaning of meditation

There are many and varied forms of meditation from the traditional yoga type to less traditional dynamic movement forms. It seems that all forms of meditation have in common that they produce some altered state of mind.

I like Eric Harrison's (Harrison 1994) description of meditation as the production of a "Calm and alert state of mind. It is when the body is relaxed and the mind is focussed. It is when thoughts drop aside, and we are at one with the sensations of the moment." Meditation can happen at various levels from shallow to deep. Harrison describes a deep state of meditation as the "body asleep, mind awake". In such a deep state, profound healing can occur.

Harrison refers to the key instructions for most meditations as follows:–

1. Relax.
2. Choose one thing to focus on and explore.
3. If the mind wanders, bring it back.
4. Let everything else go.

Meditation differs from relaxation in that the mind is focussed and alert during meditation, whereas in relaxation, the mind can be drifting and fuzzy.

Breathing as the focus of meditation

A central aspect of most forms of meditation is to let the thoughts pass through the mind and not to hang on to any. Focusing on the breath can make it easier to let the thoughts pass by. Listening to the breath is said to be the oldest meditation. It is also one of the most simple. If you find it difficult to hear the sound of your own breath, you can tighten the muscles at the top of your nose making the sound of your breath more audible.

Toning as the focus of meditation

Because toning is dependent on breathing, the act of toning can help with the focussing on the breath. Toning can be used as the point of focus or it can be background to another focus.

Where toning is used as the focus of the meditation, it can be just a sustained note or it can be a more complex chant such as a mantra. A mantra is a phrase repeated over and over; such as "OM" or "OM NAMAH SHIVAYA". A mantra may be non-meaningful or may have meaning. You can develop your own mantra. You can make a mantra out of a simple affirmation. For example; "My heart gives love".

One technique is to let the mantra develop and change during the meditation without making any conscious effort to direct the change.

A tone may have a rhythmic beat in the form of a chant. For example "Ah – Aaah – Ah". This is another form of mantra.

If the focus in not on sound, it may be on awareness of your body or on awareness of your breath. Toning may be like a drone in the background that can be the vehicle for making connections with body awareness.

Another focus for the meditation can be the vibrations set up in the body by the toning. You can focus on the vibrations in your throat, or the vibrations in your nose or anywhere else.

One of the advantages of toning is that you are actively doing something that can help you to concentrate your focus. This deliberate action makes it more difficult for you to drift off with your thoughts.

How to find tranquility in a noisy room

The art of meditation is the art of focus. It is not an easy task to stay focussed when you are in a room full of noise. It is easier to start to learn the skills of meditation in a quiet room, preferably in the company of others and with a instructor. But as your skill to meditate improves, you will be able to meditate in situations where there is a lot of distraction.

In order to stay focussed on the breath in the meditation you will need to block out all extraneous noises. If you are a vigilant type of person who is on the look out for danger, you will first need to establish that the setting is safe for you. You will also need to establish that you are not going to miss out on anything important during the meditation. If there is noise going on around you and you intend to block it out, you will need to establish that there is nothing in the noise that needs your attention.

When you are able to block out the extraneous noises, you are still able to hear the noise because your mind will remain alert, but the extraneous noises do not hold your attention. You just note that the noise is there and it is doing no harm nor does it need your attention.

An important aim of meditation is to create inner peace even when there is not peace around you.

The performer and meditation

Ideally, a performer should meditate before going on stage. The aim of this is to still and clear the mind before the performance. I know of some performers who are able to do this, and regularly do so before they go on stage. But it is not easy. Before a performance, the body is full of adrenaline and is all hyped up. The fight or flight mechanism of the body is turned on. For some people, it can be a good idea to do some form of aerobic exercise to "burn off" excess adrenaline before the meditation.

Even five minutes of meditation will be of great benefit. Remember that the mind should stay alert during meditation, so it can be a way of gaining greater focus before a performance. There are certain eastern countries where traditionally warriors would meditate before going into battle.

The art of focus

When meditation is working well, the mind is focussed on the sensory events of the present. The mind is not following thoughts, or planning, or remembering things that you have to do later on in the day. Most people find it difficult to keep the mind away from thinking for more than just a few moments.

I am one such person who has great difficulty not attending to thoughts. When I start to meditate and still my mind, a rush of thoughts come in. These thoughts are mainly about planning. Meditation is not my comfort zone. My comfort zone is planning and doing things.

Usually a subconscious part of me comes up with really good ideas during my meditation so that I am tempted to do something about it and not stay with the meditation. For that reason, I have a note pad beside me when I meditate.

I know that with practice, staying focussed becomes easier.

Grounding and posture

Grounding is the sense of feeling solid, centred and connected. It is about being connected within your body and connected to the earth. It is the opposite of floating. Using your breath as the focus in meditation is an excellent way to help you to be grounded. One useful visualisation is to imagine that as you breathe in, your breath goes into your lungs then right down through your legs and into the ground.

Some people prefer to imagine their out-breath passing down their body into the ground. Find which one works best for you.

As you focus on your breath try to not force your breathing. Let your breath come naturally even as you are focussed on it.

It doesn't matter what position you are in, providing your body is comfortable. Remember the first instruction for meditation is to begin to relax any unnecessary tension. It is important to avoid unnecessary pain. Your body does not have to be in the lotus position in order to successfully meditate. For some people, the lotus position can be painful.

When I was first taught to meditate in the 1970s, discomfort was thought to be a good thing. But lying on a bed of nails has never had a great deal of appeal to me.

Your body should feel in a state of balance. It is important if you are sitting or standing not to let your back and shoulders slump. Keep the back upright and straight, but not rigid. Allow for the body to breathe freely. I mentioned this earlier when describing the horse position.

Some people prefer to sit with their hands on their knees, palms facing up with the thumb and the middle finger touching. This is said to help with energy flow in the body.

"Esoteric addiction" and toning

Earlier on, I mentioned "esoteric addiction". This is a term that I coined to describe those people who delve into mystical and other forces in an addictive way. By addictive way, I mean that a person makes use of mystical experiences to avoid connection with themselves. This can cause them to be psychologically unstable. It is like the use of hallucinogenic drugs. The unstable person will get a high out of this mystical exploration even though it is ultimately damaging.

The addict may use a form of meditation as a way to "leave their body". I think it is fine for people to explore esoteric forces such as mental telepathy, clairvoyance, astral travelling etc. There is much to be learned in this area. But for the person who is not grounded, these activities can be dangerous in the sense of dissociating them from their body.

For such people, meditation should only be used in a grounding way.

Toning can bring a person in contact with mystical experiences. So it is particularly important for anyone who has a predisposition to psychological instability, that they use toning in a healthy way. When I use toning with a person who has a tendency to leave their body, I use a form of toning which helps them to become grounded. This particular toning exercise takes them down in their body by using low pitched notes and guided imagery to help them connect to the earth in a solid way.

Brain waves and deep relaxation

Meditation is the stilling of the thinking mind. As mentioned is chapter 10, toning and meditation can slow the pattern of brain waves from beta rhythm to alpha rhythm. Harrison (1994) describes how meditation can take a person further into a third and deeper state. This is the theta stage of 4 to 7 hertz of "body asleep, mind awake" and is difficult to achieve. The fourth and deepest stage is the delta stage which is 0.5 to 3 hertz, which is "to be awake in a dreamless sleep".

Dynamic meditation

Dynamic meditation can mean many things but basically it is meditation with movement. It can involve rhythm, movement and dancing. The focus is still "in the present". The focus may be on the movement itself. Again thoughts are not held onto. One of the nice things about dynamic meditation, is that the body is so occupied with the movement, that it is easier to let go of stray thoughts.

I mentioned earlier the trance inducing qualities of traditional Balinese music. Often dance and other rhythmical movements are performed when Gamelan music is played on ceremonial occasions. It may be that this movement to music while in a trance state is a form of dynamic meditation.

Guided meditation

The following is an example of a guided meditation that Jenny and I use in many of our workshops. You can take somebody through this meditation. You may have some soft and gentle music playing in the background if you wish.

Meditation:– Taking your child to sing. The instructions are as follows (I refer to the child as "she"):–

"Make sure that you are lying in a comfortable position, with your head facing towards the centre of the room.

Take a deep breath. Now let go.

Begin to focus on your breath.

Try and hear the sound of your breath. (Pause).

Feel your breath. (Pause).

Listen to the sounds outside the room. (Pause).

Now focus on the sounds inside your body.

Try and mask out any sounds from outside. (Pause).

Relax. Relax your body as deeply as you can. Let go of your tension. (Pause).

Go back in time until you find yourself as a young child who loved to sing.

Your child might be very young. (Pause).

Can you see your child?

Can you hear her?

Can you sense her presence in some way?

Try and find her at a time before she learned to be frightened to sing.

If you can't find your child who loved to sing, find yourself as a child who might like to sing. (Pause).

Make some contact with your child from the past. You are going to take her on a very special journey that she is going to enjoy a lot.

The sound of the background music will be with you on this journey.

Imagine taking her by the hand or carrying her to a far off place which is a very safe place. A place away from any danger.

This place is anywhere you want it to be that is safe for your child.

This will be a very special place.

I suggest a magic garden, but it can be anywhere.

Find the entrance to this magic garden and take your child through the entrance to the garden. (Pause).

See the beautiful flowers and bushes. (Pause).

Hear the sounds of the birds singing. Hear a waterfall in the background. (Pause).

Just nearby you notice a group of people. They are nice people. They are friendly and safe.

They are singing one of your favorite songs.

(You may choose to pause the background music at this point).

These people love to sing. You take your child over to join the group of people.

They welcome you and your child. (Pause).

Your child begins to sing with the people.

You notice what a really beautiful voice she has in this very special place.

You are so pleased to hear her singing so beautifully.

It must be the magic of the garden that makes her voice so pure. (Pause).

Stay for a while and enjoy your child singing. (Pause for about 5 minutes).

Compliment her on how beautiful her voice sounds. (Pause).

When it is time, take her with you and leave the magic garden.

You can return there another time. (Pause).

Start to come back into the room in your own time."

CHAPTER 14

Singing and Toning for Children and Others

Toning works really well for kids, and sick people.

Children love to be toned

Most children love to be toned. It can be a wonderful way of calming a child down, particularly at the end of the day, when the child doesn't want to go to sleep. Those parents who have a ritual of singing a lullaby to their children at night will know that a lullaby can be very soothing. Toning has the same sort of soothing effect.

Toning can be a healing gift to give to a sick child.

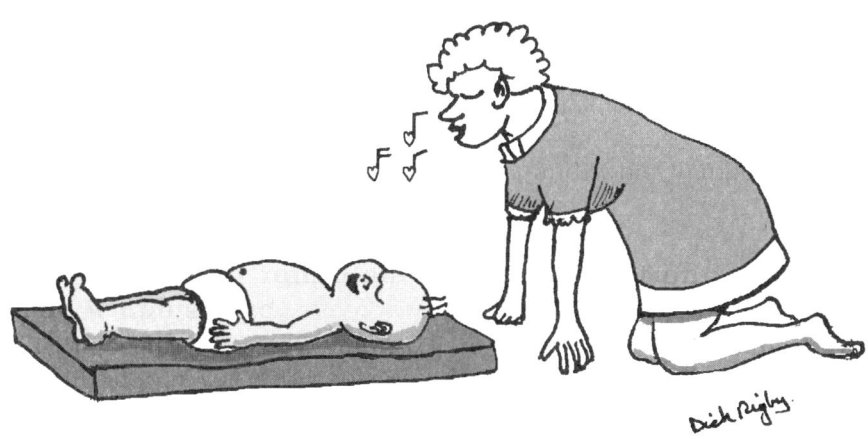

Mother toning baby.

Baby toning mother.

Night time lullabies and toning

A mother singing softly to her child as the child goes to sleep must be as old as history itself. But if this mother (or other primary care giver) believes that she has a horrible voice, there is a problem. If she believed that her singing voice would upset the child, this might be enough to stop her singing. In my experience, the mother's voice is soothing to the child even if she isn't a particularly good singer.

It is in the interests of both the mother and the child that the mother overcomes her fear of singing to the child. I have talked earlier in this book about the many ways to overcome a fear of singing. There are a couple of extra things the mother can do to help herself.

1. Sing her lullaby very softly so that her voice does not come across as harsh.
2. Use toning. The wonderful thing about toning is that it is a lot easier than singing because you just stay on the same note. You can just tone a soft "oo" to the child.

The early sound contact between mother and infant is very important in the development of the child's relationship to sound. It will help determine how they feel about their own voice as they grow up.

If a parent is too embarrassed or frightened to sing in front of their own children, then these children may miss out on developing a healthy and joyful relationship with sound. Also the fear of singing is likely to be passed from mother to child.

Nightmares, visualisation and toning

On occasions I have worked with children who suffer from nightmares. Toning has a part to play here as well. I deal with the problem of nightmares by teaching the child how to take control of his own dreams. Firstly I find out what is going on in the dream. In most cases it is possible to find this out. However, some children do not remember their dreams.

Case study:– Frightened Fred

Fred was a six year old boy. His mother brought him to see me as he was suffering with recurrent nightmares. Fred told me that in his dream a "Big grey monster with horns and evil eyes" would come in through his bedroom window. The monster would approach the bed and Fred would be terrified and call out to his parents.

Toning monsters.

The first thing that I did was get Fred to describe the monster to me. At first he found this difficult to do, but then a picture began to take shape. The next thing that I asked Fred was, what would he like to do to the monster. He said that he wanted to kill the monster. I suggested that was a bit too drastic and we could shrink the monster and get rid of it instead. He agreed to this.

We invented a magic wand for him that he could keep under his pillow. When the monster came, he would take out the magic wand and point it at the monster. The monster would shrink to the size of a match box and he could then throw the monster out the window. The purpose of this exercise was to empower Fred.

I also suggested that toning be made to be part of this ritual I advised Fred's mother to tone Fred at night. By way of this toning, Fred would be more empowered to meet the monster. Fred was also told that he could use toning to help shrink the monster.

Singing and toning the fetus.

In chapter 1, I talked about how our earliest experience with sound being before we are born. This is when the fetus perceives sound vibrations transmitted through the wall of the uterus. I believe that we should start toning our child before it is born and this is a beautiful thing to do. As the fetus develops enough to interact with us by moving in the womb, we might get some feedback as to the quality of our toning. Say, one kick for just ok and two kicks for good.

I state the obvious when I say that you shouldn't use loud harsh sounds unless you want the baby to grow up to be the lead singer in a punk rock band.

Toning during childbirth

I know that there are some occasions, particularly in the area of home birthing, where toning and other forms of music are used during childbirth. I have not yet been present at a birth where toning is used, but friends have told me that it is a very powerful experience. Toning during birth can have some wonderful outcomes:

1. To welcome the child into a world full of beautiful sounds.
2. To induce relaxation and feelings of security in both child and mother.
3. To give feelings of support to the mother.
4. To give the feeling of participation and doing something helpful for those providing the toning.

There is some research to show that mothers who were exposed to certain types of music during childbirth, required little or no anesthesia as compared with that required for non musical births.

I hope that toning and singing will become mainstream practice in childbirth situations in the future. What a lovely way to welcome a newborn into the world.

Nurturing the voice in young children

Singing is a natural thing and most children are born with the potential to develop beautiful voices. Physical and psychological nurturing of the developing voice is essential for it to develop in a healthy way. I like D W Winnecott's concept of "Good enough mothering" here. Winnecott (1991) said that children grow up ok if the parenting is "good enough". In other words, parenting doesn't have to be perfect. We all make mistakes, and provided those mistakes are not too serious, and we are open to learning from our mistakes, kids grow up ok.

I repeat, we don't have to be perfect parents.

The concept of "good enough nurturing" can be applied equally to nurturing of the child's singing and speaking voice. We don't have to send our children to the best singing teachers in the land and celebrate every time the child hits the right note. What we have to do is to make the child feel special about his or her singing voice.

Particularly with young children between the ages of two to six years, parents need to let the child feel that they have a special voice that goes with them being a special person.

We should say something like, "You sing that song really well. I think that one day you will grow up to be a famous singer". Some would say that this is giving the child false ideas about their own abilities. No, I don't agree. This grandiose encouragement, providing it is not overdone, is important in the building of a young child's self esteem. It is particularly important in the area of singing, because, all but the very best singers are going to receive rubbishing about their singing voices in the years to come.

Setting good boundaries is also essential. Encouragement does not equal no boundaries or limits. You need to be able to say to your child, "No more singing now. Auntie Jean has heard enough for the time being".

Enlightenment and fun

Don Campbell (1992 a) bemoans that teaching of music in a modern classroom has lost some of its purpose of "enlightenment and fun". He wants to see these things put back into the teaching of music. So do I. He quotes Hollander in talking about the energy that famous artists and composers have.

We all had this energy as children.

Campbell talks about the need to have us use our whole brains as musicians. "The goal is to use optimal creative experiences to enhance that which children have naturally, not to entertain them and articulate simply a logical form of musical vocabulary." Don Campbell (1992 a P 72).

Singing and toning in the classroom and preschool

In her article called "Toning Toddlers" (1994), Margi Parks talks about the sessions she runs for two to four year old children. Her sessions are for 45 minutes and run for eight to ten weeks. She teaches the parents and children breathing, toning and singing. She has reported good results in terms of relaxation, enjoyment and voice improvement.

Toning and ADHD

Toning can be effective for the relief of symptoms with children suffering from Attention Deficit Disorder (ADD), or Attention Deficit Hyperactivity Disorder (ADHD). I am one of the many who are alarmed at the wide spread, and long term use of drugs such as Dexamphetamine or Ritalin to combat this condition in young children. We do not know enough about the long term effects of these psychoactive drugs on the developing brain.

It is true that the alternatives to the drugs are not as easy. I also believe that there are occasions where the short term use of these drugs can be helpful in allowing the child to slow down enough to learn alternative ways of behaving.

Nevertheless, it is worth persevering with the non drug methods of treating these conditions. Toning is one such alternative. I will not go into detail at this stage, but toning can be used in conjunction with other behavioural management strategies to increase the attention span of the child. The child is positively rewarded for attending to the tone for increasingly long intervals of time. The improvement in attention span may be as short as two seconds, but every bit counts.

Toning is particularly effective when it is used in conjunction with rhythmical rocking or swaying of the attention deficit child.

Toning can be used as part of a program to increase the child's ability to focus.

Singing and toning for old people

Music is a great way to care for, heal and rehabilitate elderly people. Many music therapists work in the geriatric area. While I think that this is very worthwhile work, I feel that music therapists may be over qualified for the task. Skilled musicians with some knowledge of working with the elderly could do just as good a job in many cases.

Where old people suffer from behavioural problems or suffer from brain disease, dementia, or brain damage, a music therapist can make good use of their specialist knowledge in treating such people.

Toning is a technique that I would like to see used more for the rehabilitation of old people. Toning can be used to help elderly people gain focus, particularly if it is used in combination with meditation. Toning also has value for old people that feel self conscious about their singing. Toning a single note is a lot easier than singing a song.

I would like to see old people's homes regularly visited by specialist musicians and toning instructors. And throw in some professional story tellers as well.

Singing and toning for intensive care

Music, singing and toning have a great potential for the treatment of patients in intensive care. There is now evidence to show that, even if a patient is not conscious they will most likely hear the music or toning at some level. Aldridge (1996) makes the point that intensive care units have become too technology orientated leading to "a wide range of problems resulting from insufficient communication, sleep and sensory deprivation, and the lack of empathy between patients and medical staff".

Singing and toning for palliative care

Music, singing and toning for the terminally ill is an important area. Toning can help calm the patient and can assist them develop a spiritual connection. Giving a terminally ill person a sound bath can be a wonderful experience. It can be a great way of developing feelings of unison among grieving relatives and friends gathered around the bed side.

CHAPTER 15

Celebration, Communication and Spirituality

Music is absolutely central to
celebration and spirituality.
It's not too bad for communication either.

Singing as celebration

Singing and chanting have been used as a form of celebration for as long as history records. Singing appears to be a universal language for celebration. Singing is a wonderful way of bringing people together. There are many different social occasions where traditionally singing is used as part of the ceremony. Such occasions might be an anniversary, a birthday, a wedding, a family sing-along or worshipping in church.

There are other occasions where singing for celebration is not usually used. It would be nice to see more use made of ceremonial singing for a wide variety of occasions such as; the birth of a child, the opening of a new national park, recovery from an illness, an anniversary, or success at work or study.

I think it would be nice to do more singing and toning to celebrate the change of the seasons as well as the summer and winter solstice.

But you don't have to wait for a special occasion. You can get together with a group of friends and sing, tone or chant just because you want to.

The sing-along

The family sing-along and the audience sing-along seem to have gone the way of the Titanic. The sing-along used to be part of the vaudeville scene during the earlier and middle parts of this century.

More recently, some of us will remember Mitch Millar and "follow the bouncing ball". This was the era when I was growing up, and there seemed to have been more sing-along concerts than there are today.

Karioke is the nearest that one gets to the sing-along. But Karioke is amplified voice with a powerful backing tape, often with backing vocals. Maybe I'm old fashioned, but for me Karioke doesn't have the same atmosphere as an old music hall type sing-along.

Singing and toning groups

However, as I said at the beginning of this book, there does seem to be some revival of communal singing. This has taken place in the form of small choirs, toning groups, new age church group singing, folk and traditional music groups and Gregorian chanting groups.

Singing, chanting or toning groups may be anything from two people or a choir of hundreds. Whatever, the size of the group, there is pleasure in joining together with other people to make music.

Some groups are content to make their music and toning in private, but most groups will want to perform to an audience. Part of the joy of forming a singing group is to be able to share what you do with other people.

If you form a singing, chanting or toning group, think about the sort of venues where you might like to strut your stuff. If you are part of a 400 voice choir, venues may be a bit limited. But if you are part of a four to ten person group then there may be lots of exciting venues. You could busk in the local mall, or you could entertain in the local shopping complex or an old people's home. You could offer to sing at a friend's funeral or at a birthday party.

You could join a church choir. There are now a wide range of churches who celebrate with singing. Their styles range from canticles to gospel.

You may want to form or be part of a toning group. A toning group may have the aim of learning the skills of toning and voice development. It can also develop the skills of using toning as a healing tool. It is a wonderful sense of bonding when you are part of a singing or toning group making harmonies. The whole is greater than the sum of the parts.

Chris James (Internet 1998) talks about how voices combining to form a tone, produce a separate sound resulting from "a synergy of all the voices, the whole sound being greater than the said sum."

The spiritual dimension

Singing chanting and the use of harmony have been part of spiritual worship for as long as we know. Toning also can be spiritually enriching. This is not surprising since toning is very similar to chanting. Toning has the potential to help make a spiritual connection with some higher power or energy or some higher level of consciousness.

The trance state associated with traditional Balinese Gamelan music is one example of this connection between music and spiritual experience. Throughout the world, in certain charismatic churches, trance like states can be induced during religious ceremonies. Such states also have a deeply religious significance.

I imagine that a similar type of trance state is present in the Balinese and charismatic experiences.

Spirituality has different meanings for different people, but there seems to be some general agreement that spirituality is a way of identifying purpose and meaning in a person's life. To me, spirituality is the relationship between myself and this higher level of consciousness. It is a sense of connection. It is through this relationship that life is given a richness of meaning.

Singing and chanting have been used over the ages to make these connections. When you make such a connection, the meaning will depend on your understanding of your higher power. You may have a concept of a formal God sitting in heaven, or you may connect with a higher power which is "the energy of the universe", or with whatever has meaning for you.

Some scholars distinguish between the spirit and the soul. The soul is said to be that part which inhabits the depths and is connected with the earth. The spirit is said to be that part which inhabits the heights and is connected with the heavens. Spiritual toning would presumably involve high notes such as that present in Gregorian chants, and soul toning would involve low notes which connect us with the earth.

> **"Soul is at home in the deep shaded valleys. Heavy torpid flowers saturated with black grow there. The rivers flow like warm syrup. They empty into huge oceans of soul.**
> **Spirit is a land of high white petals and glittering jewel like lakes and flowers. Life is sparse and sounds travel great distances."**
> The fourteenth Dali Lama of Tibet.

Spiritual development

My own spiritual awareness has developed slowly. I believe that my religious upbringing helped blind me to finding my own spiritual meaning. I was brought up in a "good christian home" with a set of self righteous dogmas belonging to a very evangelical section of the Church of England in Australia. My religious teachers were sure of their absolute grasp on the truth. As a result of this early indoctrination, I have spent most of my life in passive rebellion against the dogmas and protocols of these early religious teachings. I was to learn much later in my life that my spiritual understanding has little or nothing to do with these ritualistic dogmas.

The spirituality that I am now learning about, has to do with the connection between myself and some higher power or energy.

There is something about toning and chanting that seems to help with this spiritual connection. For me listening to Gregorian chants sung by a quality choir in a beautiful cathedral gives me the sense of a spiritual connection.

I have experienced that feeling which Chris James talks about where the whole sound is greater than the sum of the individual notes. I, like many others, have found that a spiritually connecting experience. The added sound produced when people tone together is probably due to additional harmonics that are created through the interaction of the voices.

The spiritual connection can not only be a source of joy and give meaning, but the connection is also important in healing. The belief in a higher power and the sense of connection with this higher power can help in the recovery from illness. When toning and chanting are used with healing, part of the healing power can be the greater feeling of spiritual connectedness.

Sacred sound

Chris James (internet 1998) talks about discovering sacred sound in a journey. His definition of sacred sound is; "Using your own voice, perhaps joined with others, to experience an altered state of consciousness which is an intensely satisfying experience. It can satisfy the deep inner hunger of the seeker, and heals the loneliness of human existence." "The voice is a mirror of our soul, and like any cosmic mirror, it is sometimes very uncomfortable to be facing our dysfunctional patterns".

Original music

As you grow more confident with your voice, you may be tempted to write your own compositions. You may wish to write a poem and set it to an existing tune, or you may write your own music. You may get together with a friend or your singing-toning group and collaborate on writing a song.

Don't just think about it – do it. It can be very rewarding to write your own songs. Remember that a song you write doesn't have to be wonderful and capable of going to the top of the hit parade. It can be just an expression of how you are feeling at the time. Write the song for yourself.

It is a nice bonus if it is a song that also appeals to other people.

Music is the message

Voice is a very important form of communication for humans. There are many areas where music is the message. Patriotic songs are designed to stir up feelings and have people go to fight for their country in battle.

Music can be satire. This is the specialty item of performers such as Tom Lehrer. Music can be romantic and evoke sexual and romantic passion. This I talked about in chapter 12.

Music and toning can communicate messages of healing. Sometimes one can give the gift of healing best without the use of any words. Toning, with the intention to heal is an excellent way of giving without words.

CHAPTER 16

The Future

Singing and toning for world peace and
healing of the planet.
I hope to see it flourish in my life time.

Maybe this is the dawning of the age of aquarius. Maybe this is the beginning of a new age of peace and repair for the planet. I hope it is. I believe that singing, chanting and toning will help to bring about this change. I can't imagine this not being so. Singing, chanting and toning can be agents of healing and repair. They can bring joy and healing into peoples lives. They can help in the healing of the planet.

Toning, bonding and world peace

Toning develops a powerful bond between people. I have seen it happen so many times. It is a joy to see the closeness that can be developed when a person is toned in a "sound bath" by a group. Not only does the person being toned feel good, but the toning usually brings the group together. I have even seen people who call themselves sceptics be touched by this process.

"I have a dream!"

Wouldn't it be wonderful if toning were introduced as a regular ritual into the United Nations General Assembly. Wouldn't it be great if the Security Council opened their meetings with toning. Wouldn't it be wonderful if toning were introduced onto the agenda of world leaders meetings. It shouldn't offend anyone's religion because it isn't a religious ritual.

Toning could be an aid to the development of world peace.

Of course, in the real world with real politicians, most leaders would not want this level of intimacy and trust to develop. But some world leaders would. Leaders like Nelson Mandela would. This is why there is hope.

I do not think for one moment that our world leaders are just going to start toning. Even if they did, this would be only one small step to creating world peace. But the dream is the beginning.

I believe in the power of our dreams
and visions to help heal the planet.

Toning, chanting and particular types of singing appear to have the power to strengthen the bonds between people. This may be because toning has the ability to bypass a person's defense mechanisms.

Toning as a universal language

Toning can bring people of different races and languages together. Toning needs no words. There is no language barrier because toning is a language that can be understood by all who want to be open to receive it. Toning is a language to connect people from everywhere on the planet.

But could "the forces of evil" get hold of the power of toning and use it to harm the human race? Well I don't think so. I believe that toning cannot be used in this way. Of course, there is some potential for music to be used in a harmful way. The example that springs to mind is the use that Adolf Hitler (and others) made of patriotic songs to get people to do nasty things to other people.

Toning in organizations

At a more local level, toning could be used in management courses. It can be a way of developing closeness, trust and bonding between members of an organization. It could become a tool in the hands of people who work to create organizational change.

Toning has great potential for team building in industrial organizations. Of course, there would be resistance to having toning as a regular part of an organization's activities, particularly if it was imposed from above by management. But if it was presented as part of a team building and creative exercise, and staff members were properly involved in the process, it could be successful.

I have always admired companies who have morning "Tai chi" rituals as part of their work practice. This form of meditation can help people become relaxed and grounded before their day's work. Toning can have the same effect.

We could use more of this in Australia.

Healing the voice

The first part of this book dealt with healing the voice. I don't think that there is anything particularly revolutionary about the ideas presented in this section. However, I think that this is an area of healing that psychologists and other psychotherapists should take more interest in.

Just as we have seen the rise of sports psychologists over recent years to meet a need, we are beginning to see the rise of voice therapists. The need for sports psychologists has arisen partly from a more professional approach to sport. If a professional athlete is having psychological problems with their sport, there will be money available to pay for that psychologist to help overcome that problem.

The same reasoning exists for top singers or public speakers seeking professional help for voice problems.

Sports psychologists are also learning to work in a more holistic manner in the sense of the integration of mind and body. Voice therapist are also beginning to work in a more holistically way.

I believe that this area of voice therapy is presently under serviced in terms of giving help for both professional and amateur singers and speakers. And I hope that this book can play some part in helping shape a changing approach to voice work.

I think that voice therapy is a very rewarding area of work for therapists. As a therapist, you can play a part in helping a person to learn to speak or to sing with confidence for the first time in their life. What a buzz.

Healing with the voice

The second part of this book dealt with using the voice as an instrument of healing. There are exciting new developments and challenges in this area. Sound therapies in general, and toning in particular, show enormous promise for physical, psychological and spiritual healing.

It is exciting to think that both toning and overtoning are able to set up direct resonance with particular parts of the body and this can help in healing. I have put forward the concept that particular tones or overtones could set up resonance with particular parts of the brain, and that this resonance could influence the formation and reorganization of neural pathways. By way of these changes in neural pathways, people could heal dysfunctional behaviour and thinking patterns.

In particular, it could help with the resolution of traumatic memories and changing compulsive behaviour in a similar way to that which operates for hypnosis or EMDR.

Ecological toning

I believe that toning can be used as a powerful force, not just to heal ourselves and others near to us, but can be used to heal the planet. This is a belief that is shared by many others. It is a belief that, to the best of my knowledge, has little or no scientific basis. But what the heck, why should we let science get in the road of a good belief system?

I believe that in some way the toning allows connections to occur that act to counterbalance the man made destructive forces that are damaging our planet. We can join with others to send out healing sound waves around the planet. The quality of the toning is not important, but the intention is.

There are already thousands of people around the world engaged in sending healing energy out to the planet by the use of toning and other ways. People from all walks of life, different races and colours, different religions, different nationalities. All one people.

You can also be part of this.

Join us.

"We are one, but we are many.
And from all the lands on earth we come.
We'll share a dream
and sing with one voice ...."

"I am Australian"
Bruce Woodley/ Dobe Newton.
Warner/Chappell.

Bibliography

Achterberg Jeanne (1985) "Imagery in healing" New Science.

Aldridge David. (1996) "Music Therapy Research and Practice In Medicine" , London, Bristo, Jessica Kingsley Publishers.

Aronson Arnold E (1990) "Clinical Voice Disorders" Thieme Inc. New York.

Bandler Richard and **Grinder** John (1979) "Frogs into Princes" . Real People Press. USA.

Belo Jane (1960) "Trance in Bali" New York: Columbia University Press.

Berendt Joachim – Ernst. (1992) "The Third Ear." An Owl Book, Henry Holt & Company, NY.

Berendt Joachim – Ernst. (1991) "The World is Sound". Element Books. Destiny Books.

Biddulph Steve. (1994) "Manhood" . Finch Publishing. Australia.

Bonetti Ruth (1997) "Taking Centre Stage". Albatross books NSW Australia.

Bradshaw John (1998) "Bradshaw on: The family". Health Communications USA

Brower Harriette **Cooke** James Ruth (1996) "Great singers on the art of singing". Dover Publications Inc. Mineola, New York.

Campbell Don. (1989) "The Roar of Silence". Wheaton, Ill: The Theosophical Publishing House.

Campbell Don. (1991) "Music Physician for Times to Come." Wheaton, Ill: Quest Books.

Campbell Don. (1992 a) "Introduction to the Musical Brain". MMB Music Inc Saint Louis.

Campbell Don. (1992 b) "Music and Miracles." Wheaton, Ill: Quest Books.

Campbell Don. (1997) "The Mozart Effect." Avon books. New York.

Cheng Stephen. (1991) "The Tao of Voice". Library of Congress Cataloging-In-Publication Data. U.S

Chopra Deepak (1990 a) "Perfect Health" Bantam Books New York.

Chopra Deepak (1990 b) "Quantum Healing : Exploring the Frontiers of Mind/Body Medicine" Bantam Books New York.

Crowe Barbara J. & **Scovel** Mary. (1996) "An Overview of Sound Healing Practices: Implications for the Profession of Music Therapy". Music Therapy Perspectives (1996), Vol. 14.

Goldman Jonathan. (1996) "Healing sounds. The Power of Harmonics." Rockport, MA: Element Books.

Gray John (1993) 'Men are from Mars, Women are from Venus'. Thorsons London.

Goswami Amit (1993) "The Self-Aware Universe". Simon & Schuster Ltd. London.

Haley Jay (1993) "Uncommon Therapy" Norton & Co NY.

Harrison Eric (1994) "Teach yourself to meditate" Simon & Schuster. Australia.

Hunt Valerie V. (1996) "Infinite Mind" The Science of Human Vibrations. Malibu Publishing Co. California.

James Chris. (1997). Personal Communications.

James Chris (1997) "Sounds Wonderful" Newsletter

James Chris. (1998). Internet site: www.bayweb.com.au/chrisjames

Jenny H (1974) Cymantics Vol 1 Basle Switzerland: Basilius Press.

Keleman Stanley (1985) 'Emotional Anatomy" Centre Press Berkeley Ca.

Keyes Ken. (1977) "Handbook to Higher Consciousness". Living Love Centre

Keyes Laurel. (1973) "Toning. The creative power of the voice". DeVorss & Co CA.

Lawrence Kara (1998) "The sound barrier". The Sunday Mail. April 18 Brisbane Australia.

Lehmann Lilli (1993) "How to Sing". Dover Publications Inc NY

Lliess Patricia (1998) Personal communications.

McClellan Randall. (1991) "The Healing Forces of Music". Amity House. NY.

Mellody Pia (1992) "Facing Love addiction" HarperSanFancisco.

Millar Richard. (1996) "On The Art of Singing" Oxford University Press NY

Moody Harry R **Carroll** David (1997) "The five stages of the soul". Rider. London, etc.

Newham Paul (1998) "Therapeutic Voicework" Jessica Kingsley Publishers. England

Nutting Rosamond (1998) "Hey! There is light at the end of the tunnel". In print Australia.

Park Margi (1994) "Toning Toddlers" Sounds Wonderful Newsletter Nov '94.

Pearsall Paul (1998) "The Heart's Code". Broadway Books NY.

Sacks Oliver. (1989) "Seeing Voices." University of California Press. Berkeley.

Shapiro Francine (1995) "Eye Movement Desensitization and Reprocessing" Guilford Press NY

Suryani Luh Ketut, Gordon D **Jensen** (1995) "Trance and Possession in Bali: A window on western Multiple Personality, Possession Disorder, and suicide". Oxford University Press.

Stone Hal and Sidra (1993) "Embracing Your Inner Critic". Harper San Francisco

Sutherland Susan. (1995) "Teach yourself Singing". NTC Publishing Group. U.S.

The Sunday Mail (1998) 19 April Brisbane.

Tomatis Alfred. (1981) "La Nuit Uterine". Editions Stock, Paris.

Wigram Tony. (1995) "The Psychological and Physiological Effects of Low Frequency Sound and Music". Music Therapy Perspectives (1995), Vol. 13.

Wigram, T, Saperston, B & West, R (Eds) (1996). The Art and Science of Music Therapy: A Handbook. London: Harwood Academic Publishers.

Winnicott D (1991) "Playing with reality" London Routledge.

Glossary of terms

Accommodation (Habituation Or Adaptation) See habituation.

Adaptation (Habituation Or Accommodation) See habituation.

Addictions. Include; esoteric, compulsive gambling, sex, personal danger, compulsive spending and performance.

Agoraphobia A fear of being in open spaces particular with crowds of people.

Alexander A man who gave his name to a therapeutic technique for teaching the body to change dysfunctional behaviours and learn more functional movements.

Amplitude The magnitude of a (sound) wave.

Auditory focus The ability to sustain concentration of attention on a particular sound.

Aware Adult ("Aware Ego") The conscious part of us, of which we are fully aware, whose purpose is to oversee operations.

Beats Special frequencies caused by the interaction of two sound frequencies that are close together.

Bioenergetics A system on therapeutic body movement based on the work of Lowen.

Body Armour The way that the body uses muscle and skeletal patterns to protect itself from perceived dangers.

Catharsis or "abreaction". The release of repressed emotions in an intense way.

Cells of Corti The hair like cells in the cochlea that sense sound vibrations and supply the auditory nerve.

Chord Two or more notes sounded together which take a prescribed form.

Cochlea A spiral canal in the inner ear lined with small hair like cilia that sense sound waves.

Codependent A person who puts others needs before their own. If they live with an addict, they will try and cover for the behaviour of the addict.

Cognitive A description of the thinking process of the brain.

Cognitive Behavioural Therapy A form of therapy that places emphasis on changing the patterns of <u>thinking</u>. It also focuses on ways of changing the way we look at the world and our patterns of behaviour.

Dendrite, dendritic connection A form of nerve cell in the brain that has many branches connecting to other nerve cells.

Discord, discordant The sense of when two or more notes that sound as if they do not fit together. The notes make a sound which can be heard as jarring or unpleasant.

Dissonance See resonance.

Disowned Self A term used in the Voice Dialogue system that refers to any subconscious part that our conscious mind does not want to accept as a part of ourself.

Duration (of a note) Is the length of time that the note is sustained. You can maintain a constant note or tone for a long time by continuing to renew your breath.

EMDR (Eye Movement Desensitization and Reprocessing) A technique used in the resolution of trauma, requiring the client's eyes to follow the therapist's rhythmical finger movement. It was developed by Francine Shapiro.

False adult That condition when we believe that what we are saying is coming from our adult, but it is actually coming from an inner child.

Feldenkrais M A man who gave his name to a therapeutic technique for teaching the body to change dysfunctional behaviours and learn more functional movements.

Frequency In relation to a musical note; the number of beats per second.

Frightened Child A term used in several psychological disciplines to describe a subconscious part responsible for maintaining fear from childhood traumas and fitting these fears into adult situations.

Glissando (The siren) The passing through a series of notes without discreetly identifying or separating each note.

Habituation (Or Adaptation Or Accommodation) The body adjusts to a repeated stimulus by reducing its perceived intensity.

Harmony, harmonious or disharmonious This concerns the relationship between two or more notes. Harmony is the subjective sense generated, when two or more notes sound as if they fit together. The barber shop quartet involves four voices singing notes that are in harmony. Voices can be in harmony or disharmony. If the notes belong to one chord, the sound will be heard as harmonious. When notes are not part of the same chord, the sound may be perceived as jarring, disharmonious or discordant.

Harmonics, Overtones & partials Harmonics, upper partials or overtones mean the same. They are notes that are given off when a fundamental frequency is sounded. The frequencies of these harmonics bear a strict mathematical relationship to the fundamental frequency. The harmonics are usually heard as weaker than the fundamental note.

Harmonic toning A sound produced by one voice, where the mouth and tongue are shaped to place emphasis on projecting the higher frequency harmonics while sustaining a fixed base note frequency.

Holistic Taking into account the body, mind, spirit and soul in an integrated sense. Some meanings of the word include the rest of the ecosystem or the universe that interacts with the self.

Inner critic A term from the Voice Dialogue system. This is the subconscious part responsible for making negative judgements about a person's own behaviour.

Limbic system A part of the brain lying at the centre of the skull. It is important in the storage of memory and processing emotions.

Mantra This is a simple phrase repeated or chanted over and over. A mantra may have meaning, or be a nonsense phrase.

Memory in the muscles This concept is that memory is stored in parts of the body, additional to the brain. Information is stored in the structure of the body.

Mute The inability to generate vocal expressions.

Neurolinguistic Programming (NLP) A system of therapy developed in the 1970s by Bandler and Grinder based on close observations of people's behaviour.

Neurovibrational Intervention Toning sets up direct resonance or neurovibration with a particular brain structure. This resonance facilitates transmissions along nerve fibres and across synapses within this brain structure. This facillitation assists in forming neural connections with subconscious systems that are normally unavailable through usual verbal psychotherapy.

Overtones See Harmonics.

Overtoning See Harmonic toning.

Phobia An entrenched dysfunctional fear of an object or event, where the object or event is not actually dangerous.

Pitch The pitch of a note is the frequency of the vibration of the sound wave. The greater the frequency of the sound wave, the higher the pitch. A treble note has a high pitch and a base note has a low pitch. Pitch is usually maintained at a constant level for long periods of time when toning.

Primal Therapy A therapeutic technique based on encouraging strong primitive emotional reactions and release.

Prosody Variations in the melody of the spoken voice.

Psychophonics The process of conveying psychological information in the form of non verbal sound.

Psychotic Is a disturbed mental state in which the patient's thinking is out of touch with reality.

Psychodrama A therapeutic technique in which the client reenacts scenes from his life with the intention of healing unresolved issues.

Rebirthing A therapeutic technique that has the client physically reexperience, in symbolic form, the sensations of their birth.

Regressive therapy Involves delving into issues and events that occurred in the past. Usually childhood events.

Reiki A hands on healing technique that has become popular in recent years. Energy is exchanged from one person to another. Energy is also said to be channeled to the client.

Resonance The vibration of an object or system to its natural frequency. Musical notes are said to be in resonance with each other if they are pleasing to the ear and in dissonance if they are jarring to the ear.

Rhythm May be used with toning on some occasions. The rhythm may be part of the toning in the form of a regular pulse of volume produced by the voice. Alternately, a rhythmical beat may be used to support toning. An accompanying drum beat could be used.

Shamanic, Shaman A shaman is a person who can enter an altered state of consciousness associated with some spiritual or ceremonial event. While in this state he or she can acquire knowledge to use in helping and healing people.

Sound wave An regular alternating compression and expansion of air molecules perceived by the ear as sound.

Sympathetic Resonance When an object vibrates in response to another object. Both objects vibrate at the same frequency.

Systematic desensitization A technique for overcoming phobias which involves the client progressively approaching an adverse stimulus. At each approach the client stops short of becoming frightened and techniques are used to strengthen his confidence.

Therapeutic Voicework A methodology for healing of the voice developed by Paul Newham and others.

Timbre Is the quality of a note. Also called the tone or colour. It is determined by the ratio of overtones and extraneous sounds.

Tinnitus A persistent ringing in the ear, or perceived white noise. It is usually caused by damage to the inner ear. It can also result from brain damage. The condition can be distressing for the sufferer.

Toners' block The fear of toning because of the risk of repressed emotions being brought to the surface.

Toning The use of sustained notes to help with psychological and physical healing, voice development, and to facilitate the integration of psychological processes. Toning can be directed inwards to one's own body, or it can be directed outwards.

Tuvan singers These are singers from a region in upper Mongolia. They use a method of singing called Hoomi singing, where there is often emphasis placed on the upper overtones.

Undertoning The production of harmonics that are lower than the fundamental note.

Vibroacoustic Therapy A therapeutic methodology developed by Wigram for healing physical and psychological problems using low pitched sustained notes played at the same time as certain music.

Voice box That part of the throat which vibrates in response to breath passing through to produce the voice.

Voice Dialogue A therapeutic approach developed by Hal and Sidra Stone to work with various subconscious systems within a person.

Voice toning See toning.

Volume In the case of toning, volume can be varied from an almost inaudible ng sound at the back of the mouth area to a loud ah sound projected out.

Index

How to purchase this book

You can obtain more information about
this book, or purchase a copy from
the Dick Rigby web site:–
http://www.ozemail.com.au/~dicknet/

Dick's email address is:
dicknet@ozemail.com.au

Phone or mail order.

You can also order a copy of the book
by writing to:–
**Mr. Dick Rigby,
Kenmore Specialist Centre,
2081 Moggill Road,
Kenmore Qld 4069
Australia.**

Or by phoning Kenmore Specialist Centre on:–
Australia (07) 3378 2266 or (07) 3378 2520

About Dick Rigby

Dick Rigby B.Sc. (Mon), M.Sc. (Qld) MAPS, MAPA, MACCP, MAPPPQ, MAMTA.

Dick is a clinical psychologist, music and voice therapist with over 25 years experience. He completed a Bachelor of Science degree from Monash University majoring in Zoology and Comparative Physiology. He then went on to complete a Master of Science degree in Psychology from the University of Queensland in 1971. He has worked as a secondary school Music and Art teacher.

He has also worked as a part time professional singer and musician for many years. Dick founded and ran two jazz bands in the 1960's and 70's, playing either piano or trombone. In more recent times, he worked in pubs and clubs as a singer accompanying himself on either keyboards or guitar. During this period, he also developed an interest in professional comedy and was involved in the production of a stage cabaret and comedy show called "The Vic and Dick Show".

Since the early 1980's, Dick worked as a psychologist with the Queensland Government Health Department. For the last 12 years Dick has worked in full time private practice as a clinical psychologist in Kenmore, Brisbane, Australia. Over the last ten years, he has specialized more in music and voice therapy. He uses voice therapy to help overcome voice production problems. His particular focus has been on helping people develop the richness and power of their singing voice. He has also had wide experience in running music therapy groups as well as seminars and workshops on the development of singing and toning.

Dick runs several workshops each year with titles such as "Singing for Fun & Healing - Learn how to sing, tone & heal".

About this book

This book is easy to read and humorous. It contains lots of helpful technical information about how to improve the voice, through breathing, tuning the voice, and active listening.

This book will show you:
• How to overcome your fear of singing in front of people.
• How to sing and speak with confidence & reduce performance anxiety.
• How to control your "Inner Critic".
• How to "voice tone" for healing and pleasure.

Discover your natural voice:
• Rediscover your natural voice and develop the power and quality of your voice.
• Your voice can become a central part of your personal empowerment.
• Self express and heal through your voice.

Toning:
• Is easy to do & makes emotional and energy connections.
• For gaining better control over your voice and breathing.
• Raises self awareness.& enriches spiritual connections.
• Helps work through psychological blocks.
• Helps heal certain physical conditions & leads to integration and healing.